Handing On
BORDERLANDS OF WORSHIP AND TRADITION

Handing On

BORDERLANDS OF WORSHIP AND TRADITION

Kenneth Stevenson

Formerly lecturer in Liturgy at Manchester University.

DARTON · LONGMAN + TODD

First published in 1996 by
Darton, Longman and Todd Ltd
1 Spencer Court
140–142 Wandsworth High Street
London SW18 4JJ

The right of Kenneth Stevenson to be identified as the Author of this work
has been asserted in accordance with the Copyright, Designs and Patents
Act 1988.

ISBN 0–232–52113–1

A catalogue record for this book is available
from the British Library

ACKNOWLEDGEMENTS

Thanks are due to the following for permission to quote copyright material: Faber and Faber Ltd
for 'Choruses from "The Rock"' and 'Dry Salvages' by T. S. Eliot; Oxford University Press for *St
Augustine's Confessions*, translated by Henry Chadwick.

Phototypeset by Intype London Ltd
Printed and bound in Great Britain
by Page Bros, Norwich

Contents

Preface

'Uncle Stephen is having his car serviced in Hereford.' Every family has its own in-house jokes and this is one of ours. It dates back to an occasion when my brother-in-law decided to go back to where he bought his car and have it serviced there. As he was living in London at the time, this piece of information caused such amused shock to our second daughter, then a little girl, that she told everyone she came across for the next few days. Of course, the car was duly serviced and I have no doubt that the garage concerned still does a thriving business. In some sense, the pages that follow may read a bit like that anecdote; a random story, plucked from nowhere, followed by an explanation, and concluded with a reflection. But that is usually the stuff of which tradition is formed. It is about the way in which people come to terms with their lives and discover their identity.

This book has arisen from a number of such experiences converging together. The material has come in large measure from sermons, addresses, talks and lectures which I have given over the past nine years while working as a parish priest in the south of England. The thinking that lies behind them makes a gentle claim to shift perspectives as well as (here and there) unearth new facts. What I have tried to do is provide a kind of extended theological comment on the debate going on in many of the churches today concerning the way in which worship and tradition develop and converse with each other. In some places, this question is raised simply by having to agree on which form of service to use. This is a matter that has been in the fore-front of my mind as I have tried to steer the congregations of two historic churches with divergent traditions through the aftermath of the recent wave of liturgical revision, at the same time attempting to prepare them for what looks like coming next. But I have not offered here specific recipes for change since in any case there are often other matters for people to be concerned about, such as what is going on under the surface as worship walks out of the past, through the present, and into the future.

I have therefore attempted to journey among what I have called the borderlands of worship and tradition. This notion came to me some years ago whilst listening to Stewart Sutherland deliver the Ferguson Lectures in Manchester University in 1982, which were subsequently published as *Faith and Ambiguity*.[1] In them Sutherland set out to explore what he called the 'borderlands of belief and unbelief' in the lives of five thinkers from the modern era. In transferring my boundaries to worship and tradition, I set my sights on eight particular people who have been important to me, and whose personalities and works might serve to warm the wider ecumenical enterprise today. Any choice is inevitably going to be random to some, inadequate to others. And in choosing to write on two giants, Augustine and Thomas Aquinas, I am aware of taking some risks. However, I have long felt that some comment on their contribution to worship and tradition seen through historical eyes might bring out new and perhaps neglected dimensions of their contribution to theology as a whole.

Many people deserve my thanks for what follows. A number of friends have helped me to grapple with the eight writers concerned, either through what they themselves have written or through conversations, or both. On Augustine, along with countless others I owe a debt of gratitude to Henry Chadwick; on Alcuin, to Dennis Bradley; on Thomas Aquinas and Gertrude the Great, to David Power; on Lancelot Andrewes, to Donald Allchin and Nicholas Lossky; on Nikolai Grundtvig, to Donald Allchin again, and also to Christian Thodberg and Jens-Holger Schjørring; on John Mason Neale, to my late father, Eric Stevenson; and on Rossetti, to my old prep school Headmistress, Helen McTavish.

In addition, I would like to thank other friends, particularly my colleague Stephen Baker, with his infectious love of Augustine; and also Christopher Cocksworth, Martin Kitchen, Colin Bradley, Robert Cotton, Bryan Spinks, Gordon Wakefield and

David Scott. For the Anglican perspective, I would like to thank Stephen Sykes, with whom I share the delightful ecumenical endeavour of running the biennial Anglo-Nordic-Baltic Theological Conference. I do not think that any of them ever had their car serviced in Hereford, but they might possibly recognise themselves somewhere in the facts, explanations and reflections which follow. I must also thank once more Philip Spencer for pastoral care of the computer.

This book is for my friends. But by far the biggest debt of thanks must go to the Rectory household – my wife Sarah, our children, and our dog Alcuin, for putting up with the conception, gestation and production of this book.

KENNETH STEVENSON
Guildford
Trinity Sunday 1995

CHAPTER ONE

Journey of Discovery

ONE MAN'S JOURNEY

'In 1492, Columbus sailed the seas so blue.' I first learnt that rhyme when I was a schoolboy and I can still remember the confidence with which the teacher enunciated it to the whole class. There was a flu epidemic that affected even the Preparatory Department of the Edinburgh Academy. Classes were joined together to form rumps of a mere 20. Prep IVa was joined to IVc – quite a leap of faith in those days. Miss Broad, mimicked by so many of us because she was English through and through, strutted around the class-room with her distinctive gait. She knew well the old-fashioned way of getting children to remember something.

But it was not until many years later that I began to see the implications of that date. I took the facts as originally handed to me at their face value. When I thought about them, I occasionally felt a pang of terror at what it might have been like to have sailed with Columbus. Not the glory of discovering the New World in any case, as the revisionist historians of North America have brought their own agendas to that debate. The fear that I felt was more concerned with those mariners sailing into the unknown, and Columbus taking the risk of his life because he simply did not know for certain that there was a continent out there.

As usual, the facts are less romantic, resulting in a scenario far more accessible to ordinary mortals. Columbus did make the journey but it was no blind risk. He spent a great deal of time doing background research. He had a phenomenal memory, which he deployed to great advantage as he inspected the flaura and fauna of westward-facing terrain in the Azores, the Canary

Islands, Portugal, Ireland and Iceland. He took careful stock of
the tidal winds, becoming increasingly certain that they had to
come from a place somewhere else. And he did not ignore the
deep collective memory of sailor-folk in those islands with its
conviction that people had 'been out there before'. As to the
hardest evidence, he heard tales of driftwood arriving from
the apparently beyond. And there were stories of the bodies of
people whose faces were quite unlike anything known in Europe
being washed up on land.

For Columbus no one single item in this list provided proof
that there was land beyond the great ocean. But together they
added up to the strong possibility that it might be true. So off
he went from his beloved Canary Islands, peopled by fellow-
Genoese merchants – another circumstance to make him feel at
home. Spurred on by the trade-winds at the right longitude, and
with all the other evidence in the pocket of his mind, he continued his venture of faith. And the rest of the story is well
known, as Columbus lived that hunch of faith through storms
and calm, and reached his destination.[1]

Is this an appropriate model for the journey of faith? Faith
assuredly is a journey and the journey-motif runs through many
a prayer. In revising the baptism rite for the Church of England,
we looked hard and long at what was appropriate to say at the
signing of the cross. Hitherto the military language of fighting
against sin, the world, and the devil under the banner of Christ
had held sway in a line going back to the Middle Ages. But
instead we came up with the following:

President: Receive the sign of the cross,
             the mark of Christ crucified.

All: Walk with us in the life of the Spirit,
             as disciples of Christ and heirs of God's promises.[2]

Such imagery echoes the language of journey that reflects an
uncertain world in which the quest of faith is a lot of the
time about discerning the eternal truths that lie buried in more
ephemeral clothing. This is nothing new. The early Christians
frequently referred to their faith as 'the way', which expresses
the well-known words of Jesus, 'I am the way, and the truth,
and the life' (John 14:4). Yet this language of pilgrimage with

its images of provisionality and moving forward has a peculiar resonance in today's world. Indeed, it is no coincidence that these words at baptism should appear at the same time as the General Synod Report, *On the Way*,[3] with its insistence on the importance of drawing together the life of Christian communities as they try to reach out to the wider world and at the same time provide realistic patterns of Christian nurture. Both these activities are journeys – in which there is no exact or precise blueprint. In any case we live in a world that is somewhat weary of the slick, rapid solution to every single eventuality, especially when the word 'problem' is used a little freely.

In the pages that follow, I want to offer some observations on the journey of faith as it discovers worship and tradition. I want to underline that for me faith is not a blind risk, as Columbus' journey appeared to me at the age of eight as I cognitively learnt some historical facts. Nor yet is faith exactly what many forces in today's world would like to make it, namely a predetermined plan of action, in which all eventualities are known in advance and carefully logged in the personal organiser. Faith is rather about taking a hunch on the basis of data, in which no one single fact clinches the argument, but in which cumulatively they form a credible picture, in which reason takes its place alongside imagination, and will alongside affection.

What I mean by faith is loving trust, and I want to draw attention to a number of people who have been important for me as I continue on that journey through this life. My own journey has certainly been full of failures and disappointments, but the balance has tended to tip in favour of thanksgiving and gratitude. Early on I knew that what mattered most to me was other people, and I could only apprehend a new – or an old – idea when I somehow got to grips with the people behind those ideas. To give an example, it took me many years before I could put flesh on the mere fact that Columbus sailed the Atlantic Ocean – and that was long after I had flown across to North America a few times. In a world that likes instant 'solutions' to 'problems', part of the journey of faith is to have the patience to wait for deep mysteries – mysteries far deeper than how to measure marine life and travel in the late fifteenth century – to speak their meaning in time, and to enjoy that process.

ANOTHER JOURNEY

So what of my journey? It is far from being spectacular. I cannot boast the heights and drama of a Desmond Tutu or a Terry Waite. Quite the reverse. What has become increasingly important is not the events and people in my life so much as the way I have apprehended them. A whole host of faces come to mind, so big that life loses its constrictions altogether and I feel as if I am in an over-large swimming-pool in which there is always more space to swim, more people to bump into, more time to go off on my own and think and observe.

The first faces that appear are those of my family. Going back in time, I can think of ancestors, like a Lapp fur-trapper, one Abraham Sidenius, who lived near Trondheim, and whose son, Isak Sidenius was born in 1712. Isak went to Trondheim School and afterwards studied theology at Copenhagen University. He was ordained a priest, and died on the southern Danish island of Falster in 1780 as a rural dean. I can think of two men, father and son, both called Christian Schwensen, who ran the same village parish almost right through the nineteenth century on another island, Als, near the present Danish–German border. I can think of the firm of James Stevenson, cloth-merchants in Stirling, who went out of business over a hundred years ago because of competition from the south. And I can think of the poems of Sir Walter Scott, evoking the border-country in which I was brought up and the love of the Middle Ages which my architect-father inculcated in me from an early age. I know that from them I have inherited all kinds of different features that make me what I am, with a not unsurprising mixture of continuity and discontinuity.

The second group of faces that appear are those I have known across the years from my own environment. A teacher at school who used to terrify me until we got past the protective shell both of us used and became firm friends; the village blacksmith with his quaintly twisted moustache who used to give me a smile every day as I walked past him; the priest who prepared me for confirmation and who encouraged me to ask questions; all these, and many more, helped to shape my thoughts and beliefs. Then there are the friends and parishioners in different parts of the country over the past 20 years. There was an old man called Eric, who had little for which to be thankful after a lifetime of what seemed permanent illness. I took communion to him every month, and smoked an unaccustomed cigarette with him afterwards with a cup of coffee. A middle-aged couple who lost their son through a senseless act of suicide in the garage with the car engine left on. A mother who died of cancer with a faith that took stock of all the evidence, including her own regrets and anger at it all, and who, with a smile, affectionately called me 'that wretched man' after I visited her for what we both knew would be the last time. A young couple in the local hospital rejoicing over the birth of their baby – when the first one had left this world all too quickly. All these, and many more, are the influences from which no human being can be immune, no pastor, however professional, can be invulnerable.

But life can be full of exhilarating surprises, such as a visit to Estonia in 1993 for a conference. On the Saturday evening, a young pastor drove me out to a small town called Kose, where I was to preach – through his interpreting! – the following morning. That particular journey was like going back in time. I spent the night in a cottage with an old man who knew no English. His home had no plumbing, but it had a telephone which I knew I would never be able to use. Here I was out of touch with everyone who knew me, except that solitary link, the pastor himself. He was sleeping in the apartment which the local congregation had made out of the north aisle of the local Baltic Gothic Church (when the Soviets had invaded in 1940 they had confiscated the parsonage and the church hall). The next day I duly delivered a sermon to a congregation containing a good cross-section of the age-range. But it was the elderly who stood out most prominently, not because they were the largest group (they weren't), but because their faces showed that they had triumphed over adversity. The previous summer, a youth group from Finland had come on a volunteer work-camp to repair the roof of the church. As a kind of postscript, here was this visitor from England. As the pastor and I walked down the nave at the end of the service, local flowers were pressed into my hands. That Sunday morning still feels unreal whenever I recall it.

IN THE COMMUNION OF SAINTS

To travel in time involves laying oneself open to risk and uncertainty. So does the process of reflection. I keep the faces of the people I have mentioned – and many more – in the pocket of my mind not because I want to glory in them but because by their love and affection they have shown me that the path of faith is worth taking. There have been enough occasions when their triumphs and tragedies have proved an encouragement when I myself have undergone testings of a less adventurous kind. But they have all helped to fill a double gap.

One aspect is the gap between myself and Christ. I know that I cannot simply rely on the bland rhetoric of 'following Christ' unless there is some cash-value in the suggestion that takes the form of people I can know and love in my life now. When Paul wrote to the Colossians of 'Christ in you, the hope of glory' (Col. 1:27) he was not speaking in a vacuum. He was exhorting his hearers to see in themselves the marks of the redemption Christ has wrought.

The other aspect is the gap between myself and others. Can I find my identity on my own? The answer must always be a resounding 'no' because we are who we are by virtue of other people. The Gospel of free grace is not about gratuitous self-obsession. It is about choices, choices which are often made for us by circumstances, or often made deliberately by ourselves in the context of differing shades of grey, in which we have to weigh up what is the best that we can do in the circumstances of the time.[4] It is probably a truth that keeps being learnt that on the journey of faith we need other people's gifts to compensate for our own weaknesses, and there may also be a little bit of truth in the fact that others might conceivably want something of us in return.

I have begun with these semi-autobiographical remarks because I want to set what follows – which is largely from history – in a wider context. For more years than I can really remember, I have stood up in company with whoever else was there and professed my belief in 'the communion of saints'. I expect that most of the time the words slipped off my tongue in much the same way as I might order a coffee or a pint of lager. But the words have been etched into my memory in such a way that I cannot get away from them, and that makes me all the more relieved that modern versions of the Apostles' Creed have some-how managed to avoid altering them! But the words are import-ant to me because they point beyond myself to other people. If

I were standing up in the chancel of Holy Trinity, Guildford at Evensong, my mind would sometimes flit in two directions. One is the congregation at the service, including colleagues, the choir, the organist, the people in the nave led by the churchwardens. But my mind will sometimes think of the saints painted into the wall of the nineteenth-century mock-romanesque sanctuary, which includes Augustine, of whom more later.

The sense of the numinous is more than archaic language in the half-darkness, even though some contemporary worship could do with a good dose of both these ingredients. The numinous is about being part of something far bigger than oneself, and extending that participation beyond mere assent, through knowledge, to love itself. I am more likely to feel some sense of security on my journey if my eyes are open to the sheer wealth of experience that has gone before me. When I took couples on the eve of their marriage through the service in St Mary's, Guildford, which has an Anglo-Saxon central tower, I would invariably remind them that their first walk as man and wife to the altar takes them over ground that has been walked by thousands and thousands of men and women before them.

The communion of saints is not about binding precedent. It is about enjoying the company of others who took risks – on the basis of the data and examples that were around them. It is about the continuing process of tradition, renewed, reformed and revitalised. And it is also about living a life in which diversity is always going to be part of the countryside.

THREE EXAMPLES

To set the scene, I want to give three examples of what I am attempting from three favourite writers. My intention at this stage is to bring into perspective the importance of time and eternity, which forms the basis for much of our discussion throughout this work. If worship and tradition are to have lives of creative reciprocity, if they are to converse with each other in any way, then we need to approach our task with increased confidence in other people, living and departed, and with a strong sense of the purposes of God breaking through eternity into our time now.

Basil of Caesarea

Basil of Caesarea (*c.* 330–379) is one of the great Fathers of the
Eastern Church. He was born in Caesarea in Cappadocia (what
is now central Turkey), and was educated there and at Constantinople (Istanbul) and Athens. He withdrew from public life and
became a monk. Despite attempts to draw him into the centre
of things at the imperial court, Basil persisted in this vocation
and the *Rule of St Basil* (which he wrote) forms the basis for the
way monks and nuns work out their day-to-day existence in
the East to this day. In 370 he was appointed Bishop of his
home-town, Caesarea, a call which he could not refuse. During
his short episcopate he energetically upheld orthodox Christianity in the face of threats from other quarters. His treatise
On the Holy Spirit is perhaps his most important theological
work because it argues for the divinity of the third person of the
Trinity at a time when others preferred to see the Holy Spirit
as something less.

All over the Eastern churches eucharistic prayers (called
'anaphoras') are used which are attributed to him.[5] This plain
fact shows how important he has been and continues to be to
Eastern Christians of whatever kind. Recent scholarship accepts
that there are early versions of his eucharistic prayer in use in
the Coptic Church which go right back to him. Other versions
have either been added to by him in later life (the anaphora used
on certain occasions in the Byzantine Church) or they have been
subjected to actual revision (the Armenian and Syrian versions).
It is as if the Eastern churches were collectively saying, 'We feel
free to adapt Basil's text but we are confident that we stand in
his tradition of prayer at the Eucharist.'

One of the features of his eucharistic prayer that may strike
the unfamiliar onlooker is the way in which he sets the whole
scene for celebration in the context of history, God's history as
perceived and interpreted by human beings in their response of
faith. Here is the first part, which stops short just before the
narrative of the Last Supper, in one of the translations available
today:

> It is right, it is fitting, it is truly right and fitting to give you thanks
> and praise.
>
> Lord and Master, God of all truth, you existed before time began

and will reign through endless ages. Your dwelling place is in the heights, yet you are mindful of the lowly. You made the heavens, the earth, and the sea, and all they contain.

Father of our Lord, our God and Saviour Jesus Christ, through whom you made all things, seen and unseen: you are seated on the throne of your glory, worshipped by all the heavenly hosts. Angels and archangels, principalities and powers, thrones, dominions, and virtues serve you; the many-eyed cherubim keep watch, and the six-winged seraphim surround you, for ever singing and proclaiming and shouting your praise: 'Holy, holy, holy Lord, God of power and might, heaven and earth are full of your glory.'

Holy, holy, all-holy are you, our Lord and God. You formed us in the garden of delight. But deceived by the serpent we disobeyed your command; cut off from eternal life we were driven from the garden.

Yet you never abandoned your own; again and again through the holy prophets you visited your people. And in the fullness of time, as we sat in darkness and in the shadow of death, you revealed yourself to us through your only-begotten Son, our Lord, our God and Saviour Jesus Christ.

Through the Holy Spirit and the holy Mother of God, the ever-virgin Mary, he took flesh and became one of us.

He taught us the ways of salvation; he brought new birth from on high by water and spirit, embracing us as his own; and through your Holy Spirit he sanctified us.

Having loved his own who were in the world, he delivered himself up for us and ransomed us from the death that held us captive because of our sins. By way of the cross he went down into the realm of the dead, and on the third day he rose again.

He ascended into heaven and took his place in glory at your right hand. He has fixed a day of judgement when we shall see him come to judge the world with justice and to render to all according to their works.[6]

The first time I heard those words I began to wonder if it was possible for a contemporary Westerner to pray them with any degree of realism. They seemed so far away from the curt, matter-of-fact language to which I was accustomed. Then I began to think again not so much at what the prayer was *saying* as what the prayer was trying to *express*. For here was a means of placing me and my world within a far wider perspective than I was used to. Above all the prayer rang true with many of the great hymns of praise that I sang, like Cardinal Newman's 'Praise to the holiest in the height'. For here was a way of claiming history as part of the good purposes of God.

The second feature that struck me about the prayer was that it began with the created order. The human race only enters the scene after the ancient hymn, 'Holy, holy, holy . . .' In other words, we human beings are part of a great created order and need to see ourselves therefore as stewards of nature, not just of the grace of God. In an age that is increasingly aware of the ecological pattern, the bio-systems that are as fragile as we are, a eucharistic prayer which does not dare bless bread and wine at the Table of the Lord before it blesses God for the creation in the first place surely has something to commend it.

The third feature that came home to me was the confidence with which the heavenly orders take their place before God's throne in heaven. Basil's traditional language may not be how we would express this truth today. But I wonder if we have somehow lost interest in heaven in much contemporary worship. Somehow, a well-intentioned egocentricity has taken hold, under the guise of a human-centred, philanthropic series of values, with all the worthy, world-conscious interests that this involves. And yet to believe in heaven and enjoy singing about the union of the earthly with the heavenly is not to renounce the world, as this prayer demonstrates. Basil, being dead, yet speaketh!

Julian of Norwich

Julian of Norwich (*c.* 1342–after 1413) was a religious woman who lived as an anchoress (a solitary) outside the walls of St Julian's Church, Norwich. She has come down in history as the author of *Revelations of Divine Love*, which is her account of 15 revelations she experienced over a space of five hours on 8 May 1373, together with another revelation the next day, 20 years later. Here is someone in a very different world from Basil. For she is writing in her vernacular about what she herself has received and she takes no part in the high-life affairs of the Church.

Revelations is a spiritual classic because of its directness and its passion about the grace of God, who brings both mercy and judgement to the world. In the third part of her book (chapters 44–65) she tells her parable of the Lord and the Servant. Chapter

44 is therefore pivotal. It is also brief and therefore all the more worth quoting in full:

> God shewed, in all the Revelations, oftentimes, that man evermore worketh his will and his worship, lastingly and without stinting. What this working is, was shewn in the first Revelation, and that in a marvellous setting; for it was shewn in the working of the soul of our blissful Lady, Saint Mary, in her truth and wisdom. And how it was shewn, I hope, by the grace of the Holy Ghost, I shall tell as I saw her.
>
> Truth seeth God, and Wisdom beholdeth God; and of these two cometh the third; that is, a holy marvellous delight in God, which is love. Where truth and wisdom is verily there is love, which cometh of them both – and all of God's making. For God is endless sovereign Truth, endless sovereign Wisdom, endless sovereign Love, unmade; and man's soul is a creature in God, having the same properties, but made. Evermore it doeth that which it was made for – it seeth God, it beholdeth God, it loveth God. Wherefore God rejoiceth in the creature, the creature with endless marvelling in God.
>
> With marvelling the creature seeth his God, his Lord and his Maker, how he is so high, so great and so good in comparison with him that is made, that the creature seemeth as naught to himself. And yet the brightness and the clearness of truth and wisdom maketh him to see and to know that he is made for love; in which love God endlessly keepeth him.[7]

Basil's eucharistic prayer sees God's work in creation and humanity in history. Julian's revelation, on the other hand, is about God acting in the present. The persistence of present-tense verbs ('seemeth', 'beholdeth', 'doeth') comes across all the more forcefully in the medieval English. It is not possible to read this short chapter without being struck by the power of God speaking to Julian. Moreover, unlike Basil's prayer, which has something of the over-arching quality of true public, liturgical prayer, Julian's prose has an earthy poignancy that has its own charm.

In the first paragraph, she introduces the section of the book of which this chapter is the introduction. 'I shall tell as I saw.' Then comes the key paragraph in which she distinguishes between truth, wisdom, and love. It is interesting to observe that whereas truth 'seeth' God, wisdom 'beholdeth' God. 'Behold' is a key word with Julian. It has a fine concentration about it that 'seeth' lacks and it brings with it a sense that in such concentrated 'beholding' God reveals himself in a way that is not true of just 'seeing'. Thus truth, wisdom and love are ways of knowing God, and there is even a suggestion of journeying through truth, to reach wisdom, and beyond to love. And yet all three are God, 'unmade' – perhaps an echo of the *Quicunque vult*, the Athanasian Creed that she will have known by heart as part of her devotions.

In the third paragraph, Julian naturally places the spotlight of God's truth, wisdom and love on the human being, in whom 'God rejoiceth'. Julian always starts with the love of God and from there can move to how the human being may know amendment of life. Seven hundred years on, and in a world in which the human race is the recipient of aggressive voices crying out for attention, to buy this, go there, take that – or else! – Julian's reticently powerful message comes quietly through. For God is not so high, great or good as to hold aloof from us. Truth and wisdom are bright and clear. They not only shine but they have a clarity that can be apprehended. And the most important truth we can apprehend is that we are made for love. Julian, being dead, yet speaketh!

The Letter to the Ephesians
The Letter to the Ephesians has been read for centuries in the public worship of the Church. At Epiphany, for example, Christians have over the years been reminded of the Gospel call to the effect that 'the Gentiles are fellow-heirs' (Eph. 3:6), removing the dividing wall between Jew and non-Jew in a society that was full of deep religious divisions. It would seem no coincidence that Ephesians, perhaps the 'softest' of the Pauline Epistles over the Jewish issue, should be chosen in many churches to provide the epistle reading for the feast of the Epiphany, specifically the passage about making the unsearchable riches of the Gospel known to the Gentiles as well (Eph. 3:1–12). Not many scholars would support the traditional view that Paul actually wrote the letter (it contains too many words and ideas that are not quite his), nor yet that it was written specifically to the Ephesians (some early manuscripts lack this in any case). But that does not alter the letter's importance as a 'round-robin' letter to early Christians written in the name of Paul by a disciple of his.

Like the Second Letter to the Corinthians, and the First Letter of Peter, it begins with a hymn 'blessing' God, which gives rise to the view that the letter may have been written with public worship in view:

Blessed be the God and Father of our Lord Jesus Christ, who has blessed us in Christ with every spiritual blessing in the heavenly places, even as he chose us in him before the foundation of the world, that we should be holy and blameless before him. He destined us in love to be his sons through Jesus Christ, according to the purpose of his will, to the praise of his glorious grace which he freely bestowed on us in the Beloved.

In him we have redemption through his blood, the forgiveness of our trespasses, according to the riches of his grace which he lavished upon us. For he has made known to us in all wisdom and insight the mystery of his will, according to his purpose which he set forth in Christ, as a plan for the fullness of time, to unite all things in him, things in heaven and things on earth. In him, according to the purpose of him who accomplished all things according to the counsel of his will, we who first hoped in Christ have been destined and appointed to live for the praise of his glory.

In him you also, who have heard the word of truth, the gospel of your salvation, and have believed in him, were sealed with the promised Holy Spirit, which is the guarantee of our inheritance until we acquire possession of it, to the praise of his glory (Eph. 1:3–14).

The three paragraphs show the intrinsic argument of this blessing, as Martin Kitchen suggests in his recent study.[8] In the first, God's will is expressed in the way that he chose 'us' before all things, so that we might be his children through Jesus Christ. In the second, his will is enacted through Christ in the redemption and enlightenment which he brings. There is a strong focus on unity – the union of earth and heaven. And there is, too, a strong focus on the *purpose* of God. Finally, in the third paragraph, the blessings of Christ are made known by the sealing of the Spirit, where the writer uses the image of a mark on wax to make clear that we are no longer our own but have another purpose for another world.

When these examples – Basil, Julian, and Ephesians – are set side-by-side their differences become obvious: Basil's prayer, Julian's revelation, and, finally, the author of Ephesians' passionate faith. Style, of course, can so often distract at the expense of substance. Let us simply *enjoy* their very diversity of approach. But we would do well to heed what they are each trying to *express*. Basil is dealing with the past, placing everything before God – and the human race. Julian is dealing with the present, placing everything before God – and the human race. Finally, Ephesians places everything, from the past promises of God to the present experiences of the outworkings of those promises, in the future – in God's future. For him, it is a mystery, a secret, that is being revealed, for which he says, 'blessed be God.'

WHICH DIRECTION?
In the pages which follow, we shall be looking at the life and writings of various people from different ages in order to recover a sense of faith as a journey towards worship in a living tradition. We shall see the usual influences at work, of which the primary ones are inheritance (genetics can be as important for prayers as for human beings), formation (environment draws different ideas from people), and change (new climates of opinion sometimes require drastic action). We shall do so with the perspectives suggested thus far, namely that we are their contemporaries in the communion of saints despite the (sometimes obvious) differences of culture, language, and world-view that are bound to exist between our attitudes and theirs. But perhaps one of the lessons which Christians are being called upon to learn again today is that we cannot simply converse with people who are like us, who speak our language, and who align themselves with our prejudices.

We shall first of all see Augustine in North Africa in the closing years of the fourth century making sense of his own life through a penetrating discussion of memory. We shall then move on to Tours, in the Loire valley, at the end of the eighth century, where Alcuin, the abbot of St Martin's, writes prayers for different purposes which express an evolving way of understanding Christianity, starting with the Trinity, the cross and the Virgin Mary. We shall then travel to the thirteenth century and capture something of Thomas Aquinas' vision of nature transformed as a key to eucharistic reality, balancing this carefully with Gertrude the Great's tender writings in a convent in Saxony about the wounds and the heart of Christ. Moving on to Jacobean England, we shall look at the way Lancelot Andrewes draws together from many different elements a powerful synthesis of how God speaks and acts in the human arena. Nineteenth-century Denmark is the scene for Nikolai Grundtvig to provide a comparable 'ecumenical movement' ahead of its time, with his multi-source hymnody, bulging with imagery and ideas. Then we shall move back to England, with John Mason Neale opening up the riches of the past, including the Christian East, and Christina Rossetti probing painfully and gloriously into human suffering, and like Grundtvig, refusing to overlook the shadow side of human experience.

There will be connections, continuities, discontinuities and even contradictions. Each writer has been singled out as a creature of their own time, yet standing above context because they hold an inherent universal significance and a place in the whole Church Catholic. Each one, too, writes as a different personality, from Augustine's outpourings of self-quest, through Alcuin's precise and versatile prose, on to Aquinas' unified and somewhat startling vision, and Gertrude's human and direct speech about what she feels and knows within herself of Christ. Andrewes and Grundtvig in their different ways are temperamental opposites: the English prelate thinks and prays and writes, whereas the tempestuous Dane almost writes in order to keep up with his imagination. And Neale and Rossetti, neither of whom could stop themselves writing, look at different areas and widen the minds and emotions of their audience accordingly.

Such an assembly of people testifies to one basic truth about human experience before God – diversity. On such a scale, it is threatening perhaps to everyone except God himself who is the author of that diversity in the first place. By looking at the past in such a manner, the honest searcher can gain a sense of the Christian story driving the present on into the future. We cannot, of course, have our future predetermined by our heritage. But it is an influence that can ensure a measure of maturity, for worship is by its very nature shaped by tradition. Perhaps most important of all in this quest is the knowledge that past and present and future are all in God's hands. They are seen by him as a whole. And part of our journey of faith is to face up to our fragmented perspectives – and to keep handing them over to him as we continue to live by the hunch that there is a coherence to it all, and that the data and the impressions we have to live on are enough for the moment.

CHAPTER TWO

Augustine: Journey Inwards?

APPROACHING AUGUSTINE

> Almighty God, in whom we live and move and have our being, you
> have made us for yourself, so that our hearts are restless until they
> rest in you; grant us purity of heart and strength of purpose, that
> no selfish passion may hinder us from knowing your will, no weak-
> ness from doing it; but that in your light we may see light clearly,
> and in your service find our perfect freedom; through Jesus Christ
> our Lord.[1]

On 23 May 1993, I preached a sermon on autobiography. It was
one of the strangest preaching experiences that I have ever
known. The gospel text was part of the prayer of Christ before
his betrayal – the so-called 'high priestly prayer' (John 17:1–11).
That passage is full enough of drama as it is, with Jesus offering
himself to the Father and praying for the unity of his followers.
But I was living through a personal drama of another kind.

The previous Easter, I had been given a copy of Henry Chadwick's translation of St Augustine's *Confessions* by a friend and
colleague.[2] If I had done a 'double-take' 20 years ago, I would
have surprised myself, as Augustine was not in fashion when I
was a student. In fact, one of my biggest regrets is that I was part
of the generation of theological students who were disinclined to
look seriously at Augustine – a prejudice in which some of our
teachers shared. Every age has its own 'political correctness' and
it is not possible to take everything in at once! Fortunately, the
passage of time dealt kindly with me, and when the *Confessions*
duly arrived I suppose I was ready to take them seriously. From
time to time, I had dipped into them, but here was a clear,
accessible translation.

I began to read them properly, savouring the spiritual auto-biography for as much beauty and truth that it might hold. I enjoyed the life of the ancient world so vividly described, like Augustine's description of students who didn't take him seriously when he was trying to teach them. Above all, I found the under-lying message of a *coherence* in one's life both startlingly simple and tantalising. A personal retreat at Quarr Abbey on the Isle of Wight provided the context for finishing the book and for pondering many home-truths. With typical enthusiasm, I decided to preach a sermon on autobiography and making sense of one's life, when next the gospel for the day allowed it!

But there was another twist. I wrote the sermon in draft on Tuesday 18 May, in which I highlighted three particular features of Christ's prayer to the Father. In it, Christ sees a coherence to his life, he judges the effect that he is having on his followers, and he is aware of a legacy that he will leave behind him. And these I tried to apply to our own lives. That was what the sermon was going to say. But the day after I had written it, I received the news that my father, with whom I had a close relationship, was dying. This was not a total surprise, for he had been ill for some time – though we all hoped that the disorder from which he was suffering would be alleviated. But on that Wednesday, he was told how ill he really was. And the rest of that week was taken up with phone-calls in which he made it clear to me that the end was coming and he was ready for it.

I therefore stood up to preach that sermon on autobiography, with the cumulative effect of Augustine's *Confessions* behind me, and my father's impending death before me. It was an experience that I shall never forget, though fortunately the actual delivery only had a sense of drama to those close to me who had heard the news. Preachers have souls that have to be saved as well. We are not just in the business of pouring out our wares as if we were detached professionals.

Across the years, some of Augustine's theology had inevitably made its impact: as students, we had to take seriously his major contribution to the understanding of the Trinity. Faced with a climate of opinion which tended to start with God the Father, and then fit the Son and the Spirit somehow around him, Augus-tine took the bold step of beginning with a unified divine nature, in which the three persons share equally.[3] Moreover, Augustine's preaching – so carefully taken down especially at Carthage by stenographers – gives us clues into how the liturgical year evolved, and how Scripture was used in worship.[4] And in spite of the myths that have been around to the contrary, Augustine's view of marriage is a high and honourable one, for it is not hard to see in his writings a constant repetition of the threefold reasons for that relationship as *fides* (fidelity), *proles* (offspring) and *sacramentum* (the mystery of the union itself).[5] But even faced with the massive amount of his writing, including the *City of God*, with its cautious optimism about the established order of things precariously poised before the threat of destruction, it is the *Confessions* which stand pre-eminent because of its accessibility and directness.

AUGUSTINE'S LIFE

As the *Confessions* tell us, Augustine's life was a rich and varied one. He was born on 13 November 354 at Thagaste, a hill-town in what is now eastern Algeria, of parents who were probably both Berber by descent. His father was a simple farmer, who had a seat on the town council. He was not a religious man, whereas Monica, his mother was intensely so. Both of them wanted their son to marry and have children, but instead Augustine – like many other young men in antiquity – had a long-standing relationship with a woman whom he loved dearly and by whom he had a son called Adeodatus (= 'given by God'). His main career was that of a teacher of rhetoric, first at Thagaste, then at Carthage, and afterwards at Rome, which proved a disappointment because of the quality of the students.

He eventually settled in Milan in 384, and it was here that he met Ambrose, the bishop, who had a profound influence upon him. Up to this time, Augustine had tried various religious faiths, but two of them stand out as particularly important. The Manichee faith, in which he showed considerable interest while at Thasgate as a teacher, mistrusted the natural order of things and spurned marriage. All through his education he had been aware of Platonism, but it was not until the move to Milan that he took to it with deep seriousness. Platonism was attractive to Augustine for a number of reasons. It provided a basic philosophy of life in which the Ultimate One could be known by abstraction, if all experience is gradually divested of what is human. Platonists were hostile to Christianity because Christians believed in a God of history, and in particular a God revealed in the incarnation. Thus the two systems appeared to be pulling in opposite directions.

It is clear from reading the *Confessions* that Augustine had to take both his heart and his brain into the new faith. Various influences were at work. Ambrose's preaching and personality were central, for Augustine was the kind of person who needed to meet his equal, a man of great culture and learning, who could quote Basil of Caesarea in Greek (unlike Augustine, who never mastered the language). His friends – always important to someone as powerful but vulnerable as Augustine – provided a constant form for debate and discussion. But there is another dimension too, which the *Confessions* indicate – namely, Augustine's experience of worship at Milan, an experience which evoked strong emotions in him.

In July 387, Augustine decided finally on Christianity and realised, too, that his dissolute life would have to stop, and that included sex. He enrolled for baptism at the following Easter, and received the sacraments from Ambrose himself. Milan was, of course, no provincial outpost. It had its own local pride, it was a vital trade-link with the East, and the kind of place where it would have become public knowledge that the gifted professor of rhetoric was becoming a Christian. Moreover, Milan could boast its own liturgical traditions, a fact which Ambrose himself pointed out to Pope Innocent I when pressed by him (unsuccessfully in the event) to drop Milan's custom of washing the feet of the new Christians immediately after their baptism. The foot-washing (John 13:1–20) was not yet an established custom on Maundy Thursday, but in North Italy and the environs it was associated with the sacrament of baptism.

Now at last a baptised Christian, Augustine decided to leave Milan and return to Thagaste. On the way back, his mother died, an event that left a strong impression on him: she had asked to be remembered at the altar – a clear testimony that Christians at that time prayed for the departed at the Eucharist. At Thagaste he formed a community around him, for which he was to write a Rule, which in time was to be the model for colleges of clergy living together under a common rule, the so-called 'canons regular', who became a prominent feature of life in the Middle Ages. In this country, the Austin (i.e. Augustinian) Canons received royal patronage in the twelfth century under King Henry II in England and David I in Scotland.

But Augustine could not escape the limelight by living in such a community for long. In 391, just four years after his baptism he was ordained presbyter at Hippo, being compelled to do so by the congregation. A few years later he was consecrated bishop. This latter action was questioned by other bishops in North Africa; he was not formally elected, simply chosen by the aged bishop as his successor for the future. Augustine had his enemies in the Church. They were probably jealous of this able and forthright new convert, who had doubtless left behind him a reputation for high life in his earlier days.

At Hippo Augustine remained until his death in 430. For all that time – and it was by ancient standards a lengthy episcopate – he preached, he took part in local pastoral disputes, and he wrote theological treatises, particularly connected with controversies – for example, concerning Pelagius' teachings about the relationship between faith and works. He was well known in North Africa and Italy, and his fame also reached Constantinople, where his reputation stood high. His first main work as bishop was to write the *Confessions*, which he began in 397 and completed three years later. His other major works followed: *On the Trinity*, which he completed in 419, and *The City of God*, which he finished in 426 and which took 13 years to write. At the end of his life, he also wrote a series of *retractationes* ('reappraisals'), which were intended as glosses on his previous works, with corrections here and there. It is not without significance that the *Confessions* do not appear in them at all.

THE *CONFESSIONS* IN GENERAL

The *Confessions* comprise 13 books. The first nine are specifically autobiographical, whereas the four ensuing books are concerned with issues of importance to Augustine. The relationship between the first nine and the last four books has been debated by scholars over the years.[6] It is probably best to view the 13 books as a coherent whole, and to note the fact that there is a definite change of atmosphere and focus when Book X begins.

The first appearance of *Confessions* caused quite a storm. On the one hand, the sheer candour with which this new bishop-convert wrote shocked some. Perhaps they were not used to Christian leaders referring to night-time emissions long after deciding that sexual love had to be renounced. On the other hand, it was the very character of the last four books which seemed to say, 'I have changed, and yet I am the same person.' Surely, it might be thought, this was not a strong selling-point for a religious faith that was in many places down on its heels? For anyone reading them today, there are obvious signs of the gap between our own time and Augustine's. But the abiding impression is of startling contemporaneity. Here is a man of intelligence and strong loyalties, who is honestly searching for the truth about himself and about life. Here is a man with a devout mother who deliberately turns his back on her faith and searches through other alternatives in a society in which religion and philosophy mingle together in a veritable market-place where everything seems to be on offer, every belief is pressing a claim, and many people are responding with a shrug of amiable disbelief, even down to the aristocracy fleeing the invading Vandals in Italy in order to settle in North Africa.

The first four books describe his life up to the age of 22. This covers his early years, his adolescence, his time as a student at Carthage, and the start of his teaching career. All through, the tone is a curious blend of sublime faith in a God who is always there, walking before him, and of a tough, descriptive account of the emptiness of these years. But there is no self-crucifixion, no denial of that early life, and this is where the Augustine of mythology stands at variance from the Augustine of his own account. If God is to be found in everything, then that is a cause for rejoicing, even if the rejoicing must be mingled with repentance. As he observes near the start of Book III, 'mercy cannot exist apart from suffering.'

Books V to VIII take us on the journey to Carthage, Rome and Milan. Augustine is gripped by the challenge of reconciling Ultimate Truth with history, and seeing the things of this world as God-given, though flawed. This is perhaps the conundrum which draws him to Christianity in the end, via the Platonism that his friends knew as a fashionable and profound answer. Already the call of Christianity beckons him, and he becomes a catechumen at Milan, but still he is held back. Things seem to be pointing in the direction of a new departure in his life, and he sends his young lady back to Africa – something generations of people since have found it hard to understand, still less accept. The end of Book VIII is perhaps the most dramatic part of the whole work, for in a garden at Milan he hears a voice saying, 'pick up and read, pick up and read.' Whether or not it was the voice of some children playing a game is not clear. What *is* clear is Augustine's interpretation of the experience. He went and read Paul's letter to the Romans: 'not in riots and drunken parties . . . but put on the Lord Jesus Christ' (Rom. 13:13–14).

Book IX sees the consequences of this conversion. He renounces his professional career, he is baptised, and his mother dies. There is an added touch to the latter incident, for he recounts his mother's problem with alcohol earlier in her life, at the same time praising her fidelity. It is as if Augustine wants to ensure that his conversion is not the end, but only leads to new issues, new problems, new joys. And that is exactly how the scene is set for the final books.

Book X is probably one of the most beautiful and profound pieces of writing that came from Augustine's pen. The longest of all, it examines the meaning and purpose of the memory, which he describes as 'the stomach of the mind'. It also has some high points of religious intensity, with the cry of impatience to God, uttered on no fewer than four occasions, 'Grant what you command and command what you will.' For if the memory is where God dwells, why is not everything perfected? The answer lies in the sheer fact that memory is only partial, it is not possible to contain all that is within its scope, and therefore the unfulfilled nature of life as we know it is the challenge given to us to see the signs of a greater fulfilment on its way. And it is only at the end of this book that Augustine reaches the stage where Christ enters the picture, as the mediator between God and humanity, having 'something in common with God and something in common with humanity'. This comes not as a suggestion, an hypothesis. It comes as a direct statement of how things have to be.

Book XI moves us on to Time and Eternity, a logical progression from Memory. 'What was God doing before creation?' That is not a question to ask, since we are unable to answer it through the fact of being part of the creation. Speaking for myself, I find it is necessary to follow the sublime and at times

shattering depth of Book X with the suggestiveness of Book XI
– and to read the latter with a touch of a smile. Time baffles
Augustine – and he has to say so in several different ways. This
leaves Books XII and XIII, which are more esoteric, and the
hardest to comprehend. Book XII is about creation, in which
Augustine wrestles with God's desire for form and stability in a
fallen creation, whereas Book XIII extends the discussion on
how to find the Church in the account of creation in Genesis.

CONFESSIONS – FIVE TEXTS

It will have become apparent by now that the *Confessions* have a
lot to say about the development of faith, its relationship to the
borderlands of worship and tradition, and about the nature of
tradition. For it is, first and foremost, a work that is one long
prayer – a dialogue between Augustine and God. Our first text
– the opening words of Book I – shows this admirably:

> 'You are great, Lord, and highly to be praised (Ps. 47:2): great is
> your power and your wisdom is immeasurable' (Ps. 146:5). Man, a
> little piece of your creation, desires to praise you, a human being
> 'bearing his mortality with him' (2 Cor. 4:10), carrying with him
> the witness of his sin and the witness that you 'resist the proud' (1
> Pet. 5:5). Nevertheless, to praise you is the desire of man, a little
> piece of your creation. You stir man to take pleasure in praising
> you, because you have made us for yourself, and our heart is restless
> until it rests in you.[7]

The scene is set for a determined, prayerful, walk through
life. The determination is indicated by the repetition of the
phrase 'a little piece of your creation'. The prayerfulness is
shown by the repeated address to God. One could add for good
measure the positive approach to finitude that recurs throughout
the work: human beings are weak – but they are loved by God,
which is why they can delight in praising him. Such ideas and
expressions form the backbone of the *Confessions*, because the
author seeks a coherence in his life, a shape, a purpose, a pattern.
And the concluding words, which have found themselves
imported into several prayers, including that which is quoted
above, indicate that this purpose is best found by resting in God
himself. There is, too, a sense of conflict, and the human being
who is sinful is none the less resisted by God. Here we have an

encounter. It is as if Augustine is speaking to God, and God is speaking back to him. No gratuitous self-obsession here, but a faith that has been worked out by looking at experiences and seeing them all in a positive light.

The second text is from Book IV, when he is wrestling with Manichee beliefs and insisting on the goodness of life that can be enjoyed by human beings in their God:

> If physical objects give you pleasure, praise God for them and return love to their Maker lest, in the things that please you, you displease him. If souls please you, they are being loved in God; for they also are mutable and acquire stability by being established in him. Otherwise they go their way and perish. In him therefore they are loved; so seize what souls you can to take with you to him, and say to them: 'Him we love; he made these things and is not far distant.' For he did not create and then depart; the things derived from him have their being in him. Look where he is – wherever there is a taste of truth.
>
> He is very close to the heart; but the heart has wandered from him. 'Return, sinners, to your heart' (Isa. 48:8), and adhere to him who made you. Stand with him and you will stand fast. Rest in him and you will be at rest. Where are you going to along rough paths? What is the goal of your journey? The good which you love is from him. But it is only as it is related to him that it is good and sweet. Otherwise it will justly become bitter; for all that comes from him is unjustly loved if he has been abandoned. With what end in view do you again and again walk difficult and laborious paths (Wisd. 5:7)? There is no rest where you seek for it. Seek for what you seek, but it is not where you are looking for it. You seek the happy life in the region of death; it is not there. How can there be a happy life where there is not even life?[8]

Here Augustine is wrestling with the coherence of creation and the place of human beings as loved by God and able to enjoy him. For Augustine, this was an important cornerstone in his whole understanding of the Christian faith. What intrigued him most, perhaps, is the way in which human beings arrived at this sense of coherence. To 'return to the heart' is to realise, once again, that 'our heart is restless until it rests in you', as Book I opens. Returning to the heart is to realise where we properly belong, instead of flitting around in paths that are 'difficult' and in the end unproductive. To return to the heart is to face up to oneself, rather than to assent to a God in an intellectual manner. This is a favourite theme in Augustine, and we shall encounter it again in Gertrude the Great as well as in Lancelot Andrewes.

The beauty of these lines lies in their capacity – even in translation – to evoke a double response. On the one hand, there is the fact of God, in his love and forgiveness ('all that comes from him is unjustly loved if he has been abandoned'). On the other hand, there is the restless spirit, continuing to 'abandon' God and to refuse to return to the heart, going along 'laborious paths'. What these musings have to say to worship is that forms of prayer must take creation seriously, as well as enjoyment of God, and never forget that returning to the heart is perhaps the only real beginning of all true worship.

The next passage takes us to the centre of Book X – on memory:

> Great is the power of memory, an awe-inspiring mystery, my God, a power of profound and infinite multiplicity. And this is mind, this is I myself. What then am I, my God? What is my nature? It is characterized by diversity, by life of many forms, utterly immeasurable. See the broad plains and caves and caverns of my memory. The varieties there cannot be counted, and are, beyond any reckoning, full of innumerable things. Some are there through images, as in the case of all physical objects, some by immediate presence like intellectual skills, some by indefinable notions of recorded impressions, as in the case of the mind's emotions, which the memory retains even when the mind is not experiencing them, although whatever is in the memory is in the mind.
>
> I run through all these things, I fly here and there, and penetrate their working as far as I can. But I never reach the end. So great is the power of memory, so great is the force of life in a human being whose life is mortal. What then ought I to do, my God? You are my true life. I will transcend even this my power which is called memory. I will rise beyond it to move towards you, see light. What are you saying to me? Here I am climbing up through my mind towards you who are constant above me. I will pass beyond even that power of mind which is called memory, desiring to reach you by the way through which you can be reached, and to be bonded to you by the way in which it is possible to be bonded.[9]

In this short passage are to be found some real gems. Augustine's understanding of memory expresses everything about identity that we have so far seen. Memory tells us who we are, and we are complex – 'characterized by diversity'. Moreover, so complex is the memory that it is like a rich cave in which many different items are placed, the hint being that they are taken out from time to time, but that we cannot cope with everything at once. (Future generations employed this kind of image in order to remember complex orations, sermons included.) The memory takes in different kinds of data, such as facts, experiences, impressions, and digests them. The process is endless – 'I never reach the end.'

But Augustine does not finish there, for that would be to say that everything is well and good, and we can simply relax and enjoy our diversity. Indeed, such an approach would have much in common with some 'pick-and-mix' attitudes of today. Instead, Augustine offers the entirety to God, with his strong trust in Providence. 'I will transcend even this my power... Here I am climbing up through my mind towards you who are constant above me.' In other words, the unconscious (for that is what 'memory' is in today's terms) is not about resting in what we have discovered about ourselves. It is about using that discovery in order to reach beyond ourselves to the One who lives in our memory, and who has been there all the time. In some respects, this passage relates to what we have seen Augustine saying about the heart (restless and being 'returned to') in earlier books, because it relies on the same premise – the God of what the theologians call 'prevenient grace', grace that walks before us.

Our next passage comes from Book XI and concerns the relationship between past, present and future:

> What is by now evident and clear is that neither future nor past exists, and it is inexact language to speak of three times – past, pres-ent and future. Perhaps it would be exact to say: there are three times, a present of things past, a present of things present, a present of things to come. In the soul there are these three aspects of time, and I do not see them anywhere else. The present considering the past is the memory, the present considering the present is immediate awareness, the present considering the future is expectation.[10]

Beneath the apparent dances of the mind that seem to cavort behind these lines, we can see what Augustine is trying to say.

In human terms, we know that there is a difference between what we experience now, what we can remember from the past, and what we expect (or hope) will happen in the future. All of this is human experience in chronology and it is obviously so. But in the context of the God of history and eternity – the God who broke into Augustine's life and confronted him with the material world as not something to renounce (the Manichee solution) nor yet to regard only as a means towards the Ultimate One (the Platonist view) – we human beings live to accept the partial nature of our perceptions; and they are all bound up with a God who sees past and present and future as an entity.

The point at issue is the old one which Augustine struggled with in his pre-Christian days, and with which he was to continue to struggle in subsequent controversies. Nor did the issue go away in his own day. It is still around with us now. It is about living a life of faith that accepts the God of Providence, whose purposes are good, and yet still accept that human responsibility is a response to that knowledge – by living thankful lives that bear the marks of that salvation wrought through Christ.

Our last passage comes from Book XIII, when Augustine gives a little glimpse of what he will work out in much more detail in his work *On the Trinity*:

> Who can understand the omnipotent Trinity? Yet everyone speaks about the subject, if indeed it can be the matter of discourse. It is a rare soul who knows what he is talking about when he is speaking of it. People debate and quarrel, and without peace no one sees that vision. I wish that human disputants would reflect upon the triad within their own selves. These three aspects of the self are very different from the Trinity, but I may make the observation that on this triad they could well exercise their minds and examine the problem, thereby becoming aware how far distant they are from it. The three aspects I mean are being, knowing, willing. For I am and I know and I will. Knowing and willing I am. I know that I am and I will. I will to be and to know.[11]

In some ways, a book of this kind of creative introspection was bound to come up, sooner or later, with a view of God that arises precisely from that introspection. But he takes care to lay the groundwork first. The omnipotent God is beyond words – but we have to say something about God! And there are differences, too. (Diversity, so much a part of memory, does break out into divergence and controversy.) With some creeping caution, Augustine slinks forward with his shining insight by suggesting that Being and Knowing and Willing might in some measure correspond to Father, Son, and Spirit. In his work *On the Trinity*, Augustine develops this approach considerably, and at one stage the triad becomes memory, understanding and will.[12]

AUGUSTINE AS A STARTING-POINT

In an essay on tradition, Henry Chadwick has made the following observations:

> We feel deeply sorry for elderly people who have lost their memory. It is a rich treasury of experience for them and for all who have conversation with them. Augustine liked to say that the memory is the stomach of the mind (*Conf.* 10:14, 21 and elsewhere). The tenth book of the Confessions is a study of the way in which the memory of the past is decisive for interpreting the present. In the community, tradition is the memory of the Church's foundation and origins, and a continuing story to determine the present.[13]

For Augustine, memory is the key to identity – not just of individuals, but of communities. For his *Confessions* should not be read simply as one man's soliloquy with God. In one sense, Augustine is speaking for himself. But he is also speaking in the name of the Christian in every age. For that reason, it is a mistake to take the view that he shrugs off the responsibility to be and to act in a manner that reflects the Christian life. To have seen the light of all lights is but one step towards trying to show the illumination in responsible living. John Burnaby sums this up in a powerful passage from his study of Augustine's theology:

> The happiness which is the aim of human endeavour consists, therefore, according to Augustine, in a relation of knowledge and love, which binds the soul to the one immutable Reality. The soul that sees the Truth must at the same time see its own distance from the Truth – in Christian terms, its own sinfulness: the soul that loves the Truth must at the same time desire its own amendment. Thus the whole scheme is moralised and christened. Knowledge and love will re-direct the soul's movement towards God: its changing life will become an advance, an approach, instead of a fading away; and the

measure of its progress will be the measure of its transmutation into the eternity of that which it knows and loves.[14]

There are, however, two important consequences which have a direct bearing on the quest for Christian identity – even human identity – today. The first is about the purpose of memory. Many people today live lives that are more characterised by discontinuity than continuity. This is manifested in many forms, from a divorcee who once said to me, 'I feel cut off from my past', to a newly-reborn Christian insisting on another baptism because the original baptism, at infancy, apparently hadn't quite taken. Augustine's response to this would be to point to the method he so painfully adopted in the *Confessions*, where he strove to identify the continuities in his life first, so that the discontinuities could then be seen for what they were.

I am not suggesting that the only way of looking at life is to provide some bogus 'uniformity' that masks a whole series of underlying tensions that we must never face. Rather I am suggesting that those tensions need to be faced on their own terms, but within the context of a loving God who yearns for unity – even if that unity has to be known in diversity. There are plenty of examples of this struggle around us today, not least in a Church that sometimes behaves as if she has indeed lost her memory altogether, in the quest for discontinuities of such a radical kind that leave many believers, half-believers, and un-believers in a somewhat confused state of mind. By all means innovate – Augustine certainly encouraged that spirit. But there is no need to live in a state of mind that sometimes gives off signs of a collective amnesia.

The second consequence concerns the functioning of memory. It is not a machine, but an organism. And because it functions organically and collectively, tensions and disagreements will inevitably emerge. It is amazing how people – characterised by the popular press – continue to be surprised that the Church can live with family rows, whether about the ordination of women (in the late twentieth century) or (to revert to Augustine's time) what to do about Christians who compromised themselves during a time of imperial persecution. In such controversies Augustine took his fare share, latterly in quite a polemical vein, as he grew older and the power of his personality had reached greater

heights. The unresolved tension in *Confessions* which continues
to beset the big-hearted, broad-minded person of every age is
how to reconcile the need to recognise diversity, and how to
deal with conflict appropriately.

Augustine himself knew diversity in the outward forms of
worship. We know, for example, that there were customs at
Milan that did not prevail at Rome, and certainly did not obtain
in North Africa. Ambrose had made some significant innovations in what the people sang in public worship and these,
Augustine tells us, had their origin in the East. Liturgy can
be a conservative business. I remember once hearing a village
congregation in the Boeotian hills north-west of Athens singing
the '*kyrie eleison*' and some years later looking at the Ambrosian
rite of Milan's version of the same words. The two seemed
related, and it is tempting to conclude that Milan imported this
already-existing chant from Greece so long ago.

Conflict is another matter, and there is no case for arguing
that Augustine has the answers. Every age has to work this
question out in its own way. But the *Confessions* bubble with
enough recognition of the fact and reality of conflict so as to be
a kind of back-handed encouragement in itself. He was not an
enthusiast for uniformity in detail, probably because he had seen
enough and travelled enough to know better. But the real answer
that *Confessions* provides is the importance of seeing – collectively
– diversity and conflict in as creative a manner as possible, so
that neither tendency is stifled (on the one hand) or destabilises
people when they are trying to pray (on the other). The restless
heart has to return to itself, regain its memory, and also see itself
as living a God-given life in the present, on the strength of the
past, and in the hope of the divine future. And these necessary
tensions are expressed as Augustine pours out his thoughts and
feelings and observations in the lyrical passages of his works,
chiefly in the *Confessions*, for it is here that Augustine is being
most true to himself, true to the heart to which God kept calling
him to return.

At the end of the day, this is perhaps where we always have
to stand in our journey through the borderlands of worship and
tradition, which are seldom immune from conflict in any case.
Augustine may well furnish us with the theory, but we are not
bound to follow his practice, for we have to work it out on our

own and in our own way. This may perhaps explain why, for instance, he has inspired prayer-writers in the centuries following his death, some of whom wrote pseudonymously in tribute to him. In a recent series of poems, Rowan Williams has made one composition entitled 'Augustine'. Clearly inspired by the *Confessions*, each verse begins 'take off your shoes', as if to beckon ambiguously towards someone preparing to worship the transcendent deity, or simply coming home from the desert. The last stanza expresses that paradox of living a life of glory and dust:

> Take off your shoes.
> This dust is mine, this knotted web
> is mine, this shadow
> is my shape for you, and when
> the hot dust scalds your eyes to tears,
> who is it weeps with you to soak
> your dust to speaking clay?[15]

CHAPTER THREE

Alcuin of York: Master of Adaptation

THE COLLECT FOR PURITY

Almighty God, unto whom all hearts be open, all desires known, and from whom no secrets are hid; cleanse the thoughts of our hearts, by the inspiration of thy Holy Spirit, that we may perfectly love thee, and worthily magnify thy holy Name; through Christ our Lord. Amen.[1]

I cannot remember the first time that I heard this prayer. My earliest eucharistic diet was attending the 8.00 a.m. celebration in St Baldred's Church, North Berwick each Sunday morning. Preceded by the Lord's prayer, the 'collect for purity' (as it was called) began the Prayer Book communion service. The words just flowed. It seemed natural to pray the words Christ taught his disciples, and then ask for cleansing, before getting down to the business of hearing the Scripture passages for the day and proceed with the rest of the service.

A few years later, we changed churches. Our home was in a village which did not have an Episcopal church but which was equidistant between three towns which did, so we had a choice! In St Anne's Dunbar, the Scottish Liturgy from the 1929 Prayer Book was used, and on the very first Sunday we attended that church, I noticed two changes. First of all, the Eucharist did not begin with the Lord's Prayer but went straight into the collect for purity. Secondly, the priest began the collect for purity at the foot of the altar-steps and walked up to the centre of the altar as he prayed this collect. St Anne's has a large sanctuary, the same width as the nave, and there was no interruption of the view from the pews to the sanctuary.

That change also highlighted for me the structure and content of the prayer. I began to look at its words in a new light. And I suppose that is exactly what Archbishop Thomas Cranmer intended when he fashioned this part of the communion rite for the first English Prayer Book in 1549. The collect is one of the riches of the Western liturgical tradition, and to pray the same collect at the start of every Eucharist when there is shortly going to be a variable collect (the 'collect of the day') is a subtle way of drawing attention to its structure and content.[2] Following the same words again and again embeds them in the consciousness of the congregation through a process that is often called 'iteration', suggesting a formal and intended repetition. And as to its structure, it is not hard to detect the five traditional sections. First, the address to the deity: 'Almighty God'. Secondly, the context of the address: 'unto whom all hearts be open, all desires known, and from whom no secrets are hid'. Thirdly, the petition itself: 'cleanse the thoughts of our hearts by the inspiration of thy Holy Spirit'. Fourthly, the reason for which we ask: 'that we may perfectly love thee and worthily magnify thy holy Name'. Finally, the conclusion: 'through Christ our Lord. Amen.'

Broken down into these five sections, the content becomes even clearer. God knows everything about us, which means that our hearts are open books to him, our desires are all too familiar, and we can keep nothing from him. Because of this relationship between ourselves and God, we can dare to ask for the cleansing of the thoughts of our hearts – the articulation of our deepest thoughts – by the inspiration of the Holy Spirit. Why? So that we may love God and praise him more worthily.

But where did the collect for purity come from? The story is one of coincidences that helps to build up the belief that God is, in spite of human nature, behind everything. When Thomas Cranmer was putting together his first communion rite, he had before him a considerable amount of material: various reformed rites from Germany, Switzerland and France; a translation of the Greek Orthodox liturgy; and that with which he would have been most familiar, the Sarum Missal, which was the mass-book most commonly used in Catholic England. As a priest ordained in the Catholic days, Cranmer would have known the Latin version of this collect as a prayer to be said quietly while preparing for every single celebration of mass. The cumulative effect of this particular collect in this position cannot be overestimated.

When the Prayer Book first appeared in 1549, few folk in the congregations would have spotted its origin. It was a priest's prayer, whispered in the equivalent of the sacristy, though it would have been familiar in another English version to readers of *The Cloud of Unknowing*, that masterpiece of fourteenth-century devotion, where it comes at the start of the prologue.[3]

But how did it get into the Sarum mass? We do not know exactly who was responsible. What we *do* know is that this collect had been used for centuries in conjunction with other prayers at masses 'for the purification of the heart by asking for the Holy Spirit' (to give its full title). And someone must have picked it out of the considerable repertoire of mass-prayers for different occasions and given it its new and prominent position in the piety of the clergy. Because new ideas get tried out before they become enshrined in print – or, in this case, copied out in manuscript – I suspect that this collect was recited by heart before mass and became a fashion, like so many other things. Stephen Sykes in a revealing essay has drawn attention to what he calls 'the open heart' in Cranmer's writings, starting with our collect. It is indeed arresting that the word 'heart' should have such prominence, not only in the collect itself, but also in the title of the mass-set itself. The heart is – in the biblical tradition – the seat of the personality. Here, once again, I would go further and suggest a continuity with Augustine's 'return to the heart', the true self, the real person, the part of oneself which it is not ultimately possible to deceive without doing lasting damage to one's life. Moreover, the 'heart' that is to be open – and then cleansed – is the corporate heart of the whole Church, the entire human race, as it awaits the revelation of truth in the unfolding pattern of life.[4]

And who wrote the collect? One has to travel further back in history still, to the time of Charlemagne (*c.* 742–814). As he built up his western empire, he was faced with the need to govern the Church effectively, and this meant imposing some kind of liturgical and educational order. Faced with local liturgical uses of different kinds, he sent a messenger to Pope Hadrian I in Rome and asked for a copy of the form of mass as used by his famous predecessor Pope Gregory the Great (*c.* 540–604). Hadrian seems not to have been greatly sympathetic to Charlemagne's request for liturgical regulation, but eventually a copy did arrive, which posed the added problem of how to adapt it for use in his kingdoms, which consisted of what we now call France, northern Spain, the Low Countries, the western parts of Germany, Austria and much of Italy. Charlemagne had romantic ambitions for his terrain, and was himself crowned as emperor by the Pope in 800. Clearly some adaptation was required. Although the main part of the work was accomplished by Benedict of Aniane (*c.* 750–821), a zealous reforming monk from the south of France, we do know that a small contribution to it was made by one of Charlemagne's ablest courtiers, one Alcuin of York.

WHO WAS ALCUIN OF YORK?[5]

Alcuin was born in Northumbria around the year 732 and he came from the nobility. He inherited some land near Spurn Point, where a Saxon monk called Wilgils had gone to live as a hermit. Such was the fame of this monk that the King of Northumbria gave him land on which to build a monastery. At an early age, perhaps as early as eight, Alcuin was sent to York for his education and it was here, for the next 40 years, that he based his life, which explains the deep affection he had for the place right to the end of his life. He was a fine scholar and helped to build up the library at York, under Albert, who became archbishop in 767. Alcuin and Albert were close friends and the new archbishop immediately put the Northumbrian scholar, with another colleague called Eanbald, in charge of building a new church, as the old Saxon Minster had been burnt down by the Danes in 741.

Alcuin would probably have stayed at York right through to the end of his life, but one of those accidents of history got in the way. Eanbald became archbishop in 778 on the death of Albert, and three years later Alcuin was chosen to travel to Rome to ask the Pope to grant Eanbald the right to wear the *pallium*, which was a stole-like vestment worn over the chasuble at Mass, traditionally made from lamb's wool, and regarded as the personal gift of the Pope to established archbishops. On his way back from Rome, Alcuin met Charlemagne at Parma (they had already encountered each other on one of Alcuin's previous visits to the Continent). The Emperor immediately identified Alcuin as an able cleric who could take his proper part in the new order.

Accordingly, Charlemagne asked Alcuin to leave his life at York behind and teach at the palace school at Aachen, which was virtually Charlemagne's capital.

For the next 14 years, Alcuin worked under Charlemagne at Aachen and at other places in the empire. His duties included training a fresh generation of scholars at a time when learning was at a low ebb. That meant taking a full part in what has been called the 'Carolingian renaissance', which affected many aspects of daily living, down to the 'Carolingian script', with its carefully wrought, square figures, which Alcuin himself is supposed to have perfected. The standard of training for the clergy was raised. Liturgical music was given the same treatment as the mass, with increased Romanisation of the more elaborate, varied native form of the chant, again at Charlemagne's encouragement. Above all, Alcuin's position at Aachen placed him near the centre of power. Unlike Augustine, who was a somewhat larger-than-life figure, Alcuin was the perfect courtier. The style of his letters shows a gentle firmness, ready to encourage, but also ready – when necessary – to take a stand. It is clear from the correspondence that Alcuin and Charlemagne were good friends. They were of a similar age, and the Northumbrian scholar must have instinctively realised that to work in the new context was the chance of a lifetime.

In 796, however, Alcuin was surprised to be appointed abbot of St Martin of Tours, where he remained until his death in 804. Probably the most important religious house in France at the time, this was where St Martin (*c.* 397), the famous soldier-turned missionary, was buried. The abbey also owned considerable property. It is said that the monks themselves needed more discipline. Perhaps Alcuin was given this prestigious post to discourage him from wanting to return in his old age to his beloved York. His gentle firmness, in any case, had met with an unusual reward.

ALCUIN'S WORKS

Alcuin's literary output was considerable. Apart from his many letters – for example, the one written a few years before his death to Charlemagne, refusing to travel from Tours to Aachen because of his declining health – he wrote Latin verse of high quality. But his liturgical work is what we are concerned with here, and it comes in three main categories.

First of all, we have his mass-prayers. These date from his time at Tours, and they were written down in the Sacramentary (mass-book) of the abbey, two copies of which are extant, dating from the end of the ninth century. But the importance of these prayers is not their originality so much as that they form part of a living tradition. Alcuin adapted what he inherited, and this can be seen throughout his liturgical works.

The list of masses which bears his name makes interesting reading, for it shows the way in which the Eucharist was changing in its manner and context of celebration. And these masses are all the more remarkable for having been written – or compiled from other sources – by an abbot who was not a priest. Each mass-set consisted not only of the collect of the day, but also of a prayer over the oblations (at the offertory); a proper preface during the eucharistic prayer (where appropriate); a post-communion prayer; and a prayer over the people at the end (a quasi-blessing – the formal blessing was a development yet to come).

Here are Alcuin's masses: the Trinity; Wisdom; the Holy Cross; the Virgin Mary; for the help of the angels; in honour of All Saints; for the veneration of the relics of the saints deposited in the altar; in the church of any martyr or confessor; for the priest himself (in the first person singular); for one's own family; for Love; for purification of the heart by the Holy Spirit (from which the 'collect for purity' is derived); for the Holy Spirit; for the gift of tears; for a living friend; for living friends; for penitents; for sins; for departed brothers; for the faithful departed; for the departed in general; for the salvation of the living and departed.[6]

Such a collection of mass-prayers shows a shift in two directions. One is that the Eucharist becomes celebrated with particular theological mysteries in mind – for example, the Trinity, the cross and the angels. The other is focused on specific concerns of the community of a pastoral kind, such as the gift of tears. As one reads through the list, one can see how the first flows naturally into the second in a natural manner, perhaps indicating the turn of mind that produced the list in the first place. There was nothing new about thinking of the Trinity or a departed brother in the community: it is the composition of such a list which is of intrinsic interest. God and the human race meet on all fronts in a carefully circumscribed community, starting with divine nature and travelling through various kinds of human need. That mass for the gift of tears has prayers for the opening up of human emotions and repeats the cleansing and forgiving power of the Holy Spirit. And one may celebrate the Eucharist with intention for the departed who are to be remembered – as Monica besought Augustine when she was dying. When were these prayers used? It appears that the first few were used on established week-days in the season after Pentecost, headed up by the Trinity prayers on the Sunday following. This gives us the germ of what later came to be called Trinity Sunday. We shall be looking at the Trinity mass-prayers later.

The second area of Alcuin's work which needs noting is his *De Laude Dei* (= 'On the Praise of God'), which was written about the year 790.[7] This is a devotional anthology whose fourth book contains no fewer than 93 antiphons to the Virgin Mary. The collection is doubly important, for it shows that the cult of the Virgin Mary was strong in England at the time, and the antiphons themselves come from different parts of Europe, which fact alone bears testimony to Alcuin's ability to collect material from diverse sources. We have seen how Alcuin placed his Trinity mass first on the list of special masses. Here is a comparable concern for the incarnation through the festivals of the Virgin Mary which had been introduced at Rome at the end of the seventh century, the purification (2 February), the annunciation (25 March), the assumption (15 August) and the nativity (8 December). The language of these antiphons is both lavish and carefully composed, for they point to the fundamental truth that the Virgin Mary is the 'God-bearer' (*theotokos* in the Greek tradition). Here are some of these verses:

> She is made the gate of heaven, the Virgin Mother is made the daughter of God.

> Blessed are you among women, through whom the curse of the mother Eve is dissolved.

> Rejoice and be glad, O blessed mother of God, who by your truly virginal hospitality obtained for us the favour of the Lord who is feared in heaven, earth and hell.

We praise you, O glorious one, we glorify you, you are crowned
with the crown of the kingdom, intercede for us, for you are blessed.

For the twentieth-century reader, there may be a dividing-
line in these antiphons between those which would be acceptable
to people with Protestant sympathies and those which would
not. For example, while the first three are direct addresses to
the Virgin Mary which point to her role in the incarnation of the
Son of God, the fourth goes further and seeks her intercession,
which had already been common custom in East and West for
some time. But we cannot fail to recognise two vital dimensions
to the formation of worship and tradition through prayer. One
is the need to root Jesus Christ in history as the incarnate Son
of God, hence the place of his mother in our own contemplation
– and worship. The other is to feel the warmth of these venerable
texts, which exude a sense of pleasure and intimacy which suggest
that their original authors actually enjoyed writing them.

The third and final area of Alcuin's work comes from his
devotional prayers.[8] Here once again we are faced with a tran-
sition which is part of a tension that Christians seem to have
lived with in one way or another from the beginning. Is prayer
corporate or individual? Should we read prayers that are written
in the plural when we are on our own? In what sense does the
community relate to the individual?

These are questions that are never entirely settled, because
Christian life is often in a permanent state of shifting between
these polarities. The prayers Alcuin wrote show the variation.
Here is one of the invocations of the Trinity:

> Lord God almighty, eternal, ineffable, without end and without
> beginning, whom we confess as one in trinity and threefold in unity.
>   You alone I adore, I praise, I glorify. And to you I render thanks
> as pitiful and gentle who granted me to be taken away from the
> night of perfidy and error in order to share in your grace.
>   Complete, I pray you, the work of mercy you have begun in me,
> and grant me to think, speak and do what is pleasing to you. Watch
> over me with your affection so freely given, and make me, unworthy
> and wretched as I am, to come to see you face to face.

This prayer is addressed to all three persons of the Trinity. It
begins with a corporate dimension ('we confess') but soon slips
into the intended singular. There is a faint echo of the *Gloria in*

excelsis in the second paragraph ('adore', 'praise', 'glorify', 'render thanks'), which is perhaps extended by the plea for mercy, and the concluding vision of heaven. Not perhaps a composition of the highest order, it none the less expresses something of the deep piety of a personal kind which flourished at the time.

Much more could be said about Alcuin's liturgical work. We now turn to look in more detail at his Trinity mass-prayers.

ALCUIN AND THE TRINITY[9]

The texts of the original version are as follows, in English translation:

Collect

> Almighty and everlasting God, you have given your servants grace in the confession of a true faith to acknowledge the glory of the Trinity, and in the power of your majesty to worship the unity. Grant that by steadfastness in this faith we may be defended from all adversities; through Jesus Christ our Lord.

Prayer over offerings

> Lord our God, sanctify, we pray, through the invocation of your holy name, the offering of this oblation, and by it make ourselves an eternal gift to you.

Proper preface

> It is truly fitting and proper, right and profitable to our salvation, that we should at all times and in all places give thanks to you, Lord, holy Father, almighty and everlasting God. Who with your only-begotten Son and the Holy Spirit are one God, and one Lord. Not in the individuality of a single person, but in the Trinity of one substance. For what we believe from your revelation concerning your glory, the same also do we believe of your Son and of the Holy Spirit, without any difference or separation. So that in confessing the true and everlasting Godhead, we shall adore distinction in persons, oneness in being, and equality in majesty, which the Angels and Archangels, the Cherubim also and the Seraphim do praise, never ceasing to cry out as with one voice. . . 'Holy, Holy, Holy. . .'

Post communion

> May the receiving of this sacrament, Lord our God, and the
> acknowledging of the holy and eternal Trinity in its indivisible unity,
> be profitable to us for the salvation of both body and soul.

The first point that needs to be said about these prayers is
that they are abstract in their language. Alcuin was a great
admirer of Augustine, and there are indirect influences of Augustine's Trinitarian theology in these prayers. The proper preface
comes from another, earlier source, the so-called 'Gelasian' Sacramentary. This was a version of the Roman liturgy, lightly
adapted, and recently copied down in a convent at Chelles, near
Paris. The preface is supposed to be used on the Sunday of the
octave of Pentecost but there are no obviously Trinitarian motifs
in the other prayers at this mass. It would appear, then, that
Alcuin began the process of conceiving Trinity Sunday by using
this preface as the inspiration for his other prayers at this mass.

There seems to have been a Trinitarian spirit around as time
went on. Rabanus Maurus (776–856), who ultimately became
Archbishop of Mainz, was taught by Alcuin at Tours and took
all his mass-prayers with him to Fulda, where he became abbot.
The abbey at Fulda became a centre of culture and education
in the empire, so that what was used there mattered. In the
'Fulda Sacramentaries' from the tenth and eleventh centuries,
Alcuin's Trinity mass appears in full not only for the first Sunday
after Pentecost but also at the head of the list of 'votive' masses,
but with an impressive iconographic device depicting Christ in
majesty as the One through whom the Trinity is revealed.

Further, these Trinity mass-prayers were used from the twelfth
century onwards in many parts of northern Europe at the nuptial
Eucharist. In other words, they were considered so important
that they were brought into the marriage service, since those
who were married in church had a nuptial mass. As to Trinity
Sunday itself, it was not until 1251, when Pope Innocent IV
visited Holy Trinity Church, Cracow, that the feast was given
some recognition, and in the following century, in 1334, it was
extended to the whole Western Church. One barometer of
enduring enthusiasm for the feast is how the remaining Sundays
of the year should be reckoned. At Rome, it was 'after Pentecost',
but elsewhere, including England, it was 'after Trinity'.

Nor is the tale confined to Trinity Sunday or nuptial masses. We encounter in late Anglo–Saxon prayer-books forms of the Office of the Trinity which were in common use together with Offices of the Holy Cross and the Virgin Mary alongside the regular hours of prayer, but probably intended for regular use by monks who had responsibilities which took them away from the abbey. At the New Minster at Winchester (the Cathedral's predecessor), there was a monk called Aelfwine, who may have been responsible for outlying lands or priories belonging to his community. Because he had to travel around a great deal, he had one of these books, which has been edited recently and dated to around the year 1030. It is clear that the form of Trinity Office which Aelfwine used relied considerably on Alcuin's prayers, both in the collects and in the more lengthy devotional prayers at the end.[10] And one cannot fail to notice the correspondence between these three Offices – the Trinity, the Holy Cross, and the Virgin Mary – with Alcuin's list of masses, which has Trinity first, and the Cross and the Virgin Mary in third and fourth place. These theological mysteries were of importance at the time and were explored and celebrated in this way.

ALCUIN'S CONTRIBUTION

We may express Alcuin's contribution directly from what we have so far seen. It concerns the pastoral context in which the Eucharist is celebrated; the focus of the Virgin Mary; the role of private devotion in relation to public prayer; and the doctrine of the Trinity itself.

First of all, the pastoral context of the Eucharist. We saw the series of masses which he compiled for daily use in the abbey at Tours, a list which he commended to other monasteries as well, and which survived into later books with remarkable strength. What his list embodies is a way of looking at the life of faith in a perspective that may seem distant from us but which met the needs of the time. Doctrines of God, in the Trinity and in redemption (the cross), lead into the angels and the saints. Then comes the church building, and its particular dedications (including, presumably, side-altars), followed by the local community. The mass of love heads up the little group of celebrations about virtues, including the Holy Spirit, and the gift of tears. This last mass then turns the focus on pastoral concerns, friends

living, penitent, sinful, and departed. It is almost as if Alcuin
were constructing his own way of understanding the whole
Church Catholic, as he begins with the Trinity and ends with
the departed.

Alcuin was, however, only part of a wider process in which
others had their part to play. Benedict of Aniane was the more
influential of Charlemagne's liturgical advisers. He was responsible to bringing some order into the Benedictine communities
in the new empire. As far as the liturgy is concerned, he swamped
Alcuin's list by introducing many more directly pastoral inten-
tions for specific necessities. These include masses in times of
fasting, pestilence, crop-failure and tribulation, and numerous
different kinds of masses for the dead. We have already hinted
at the disputes which surfaced at the Reformation. Doctrines of
God and Christ deserve prominence in the rest of the liturgy in
any case; and specific necessities are usually dealt with in the
intercession. But as we are discovering today, that solution is
not entirely satisfactory either. In an age which has produced
more eucharistic prayers perhaps than ever before, it would seem
that the repertoire of what we can say about God and the work
of Christ in public prayer is unlimited! Perhaps that is what
Alcuin was trying to say, too, by compiling those masses. It is
something of an irony that the collect from the mass for the
purification of the heart should have found its place in the hearts
of Anglicans all over the world simply because Thomas Cranmer
knew it – and doubtless loved it – as a prayer for a priest to
recite on his own just before beginning mass.

And what of those 'necessities'? In Alcuin's time, the prayer
of the faithful (the intercession) had already all but disappeared,
so that the rest of the Eucharist had somehow to 'carry' the
pastoral needs of the community. In our own day, the intercessions often seem like a series of facts and no more. People
actually talk of items of prayer being 'given out in church' as if
the community needed an extra news bulletin. Perhaps there is
no way round this issue, which stems from the desire of a
community to pray in specific, realistic terms for the sick, the
sorrowful, the departed. But I wonder if some of Alcuin's concerns, like angelic help and the cross, and even the gift of
tears, might give some depth and weight to public worship and
Christian living today.

Then we come to the Virgin Mary, Alcuin did not invent any of the antiphons which we quoted as examples of liturgical prayer at the time. But he collected them together in order to foster a living tradition. There are, too, some sensitivities over whether or not it is legitimate to ask for her prayers. For some Christians, that is the most natural thing in the world. For others, such a practice is so repugnant that *any* mention of the Virgin Mary in public or private prayer – except perhaps at Christmas time! – is unthinkable. Yet Alcuin's enthusiasm for the Virgin Mary needs to be seen in the wider context of his vision of the communion of all saints; hence his mass-prayers for that mystery, which helped to popularise a regular Eucharist with that primary focus in the ensuing centuries.

The controversies of those centuries are all too familiar. And yet I wonder whether in those Anglo–Saxon antiphons there is not something profoundly Christian that many people on either side of the great divide may be missing. For too many Protestants, Mary is regarded as a dead Roman Catholic. By the simple mode of direct address – 'Rejoice, Virgin Mary' – there is a means of crossing that divide and concentrating on that which should unite all Christians. Much of the warmth which people find missing in contemporary worship may perhaps be made up for by a proper attention to the Virgin Mary as the God-bearer, the first of the redeemed, the one to whom the Lord committed his beloved disciples at the cross (John 19:26).[11]

The question of individual devotion is a vexed one today. Alcuin knew the importance of prayers of this kind, and we noted how 200 years after his death, an Office of the Trinity used by a monk of Winchester was part of an obvious trend. Such an Office would include opening versicles, psalmody, canticles, a hymn, a short reading, short prayers with responses, and would end with a series of collects. But these collects led immediately into individual prayers, in the first person singular. I wonder if these were not considered the heart of the Office in question, with all their passion and simplicity.

In today's world, where public worship has to carry a heavy burden in people's spiritual lives, and where often the prayers that are used lack the 'affective' dimension which many of our hymns manage to embody without difficulty, there is a crying need for a reappraisal of precisely this aspect of Christian faith.

As we shall see with Gertrude and Andrewes, devotional prayer of such an affective kind steadfastly refuses to give up in the face of the more austere, corporatist prayers of the public liturgy. All traditions know the interplay of these approaches. I wonder if some of the more personal reflections which are often inserted by members of our congregations into the intercessions are not a kind of coded request for more of this piety when the crowd assembles on Sunday mornings.

Then there is the Trinity. In Alcuin's time, there were rival views, which included those who wanted to subordinate the Son as only 'adopted' by the Father. It gave Alcuin a particular enthusiasm for the Apostles' Creed; and we know that the Nicene Creed was gradually establishing its position in the Eucharist around this time. But it is possible that the Trinity was becoming so strong in popular piety that it was even reflected in local coinage. We know that in about 810 a silver penny with a 'triple aura' was struck for King Cenwulf of Mercia in Canterbury by a moneyer called Sighebert. This device looks like three equilateral triangles, with sides curving gently inwards, superimposed on three circles; the effect is to give the impression of 'three-together'. The triple aura is traditionally associated with Christ in glory, an expression in abstract form of the 'Christ in majesty' depicted in the Fulda Sacramentaries, which we noted earlier.[12]

It may be that Alcuin's prayers definitely antedate this coinage device. In any case, Augustine's approach to Trinitarian theology lies behind Alcuin's thought, and such a 'triple aura' is a strong icongraphic expression of Augustine's approach to the Trinity as it shines forth to humanity in perfect and equal form. Towards the end of his life, Alcuin wrote a short work on the Trinity which owes a great deal to Augustine's far more lengthly writings on the subject, which echoes the ideas expressed in his prayers, including the power of God's majesty and the protection that this extends. That theme of protection runs through into the choice of gospel reading often used with this mass – the coming of the Spirit, to keep the disciples from falling away (John 15:26–27; 16:1–4).[13]

But is there something missing? The language is abstract and it has been taken over into the Book of Common Prayer, since the collect for Trinity Sunday is a Cranmerian version of the collect quoted earlier. Alcuin's language has been supplemented by an approach which engages the human race more directly. In the 1970 Roman Missal's mass of the Trinity, Alcuin's preface and other prayers have been edited slightly, but the collect has been replaced by a new composition:

> Father, you sent your Word to bring us truth, and your Spirit to make us holy. Through them we come to know the mystery of your life. Help us to worship you, one God in three Persons, by proclaiming and living our faith in you.

The Church of England's *Alternative Service Book* (1980) has been more cautious and provides two collects, which usually means that the first is used as the collect of the day and the second as a prayer after communion. It is this second prayer which is the new composition, which is a more succinct and elegant alternative than the new Roman Catholic text:

> Almighty and eternal God, you have revealed yourself as Father, Son and Holy Spirit, and live and reign in the perfect unity of love. Hold us firm in this faith, that we may know you in all your ways, and evermore rejoice in your eternal glory, now and for ever.[14]

Theologies of the Trinity, as Augustine knew well, are not the easiest of things to get right. Alcuin's devotion to the Holy Spirit perhaps explains why in the epistle-lectionary that bears his name it is Paul's discourse on many gifts but one Spirit (1 Cor. 12:2–11) that is to be read on the Sunday after Pentecost, whereas the other extant lectionaries all direct John's vision of heaven (Rev. 4).[15] What we note of Alcuin's language is that for all its measured beauty ('in the power of the majesty to worship the unity') it lacks the sense of human involvement in the life of redemption, other than in passive terms. Perhaps passivity is something Christians today find difficult. On the other hand, to balance this attitude, we do have the devotional prayer which we discussed, in which the individual gazes at the Trinity and asks God to 'watch over me with your affection, freely given, and make me, unworthy and wretched that I am, to come to see you face to face.'

From all this, Alcuin emerges as a man of imaginative adaptation. For a tradition to be a living one, which can nourish and profit the faithful seeker, this is gift to be prized and valued. And above all, it is a quality that is needed if the borderlands of worship and tradition are to be adequately explored.

CHAPTER FOUR

Two Thirteenth-Century Contrasts:
Thomas Aquinas and Gertrude the Great

Thomas Aquinas

THE CORPUS CHRISTI COLLECT

O Lord Jesus Christ, who in a wonderful sacrament hast left unto us a memorial of thy passion: Grant us, we beseech thee, so to venerate the Sacred Mysteries of thy Body and Blood, that we may ever perceive within ourselves the fruit of thy redemption; who livest and reignest with the Father in the unity of the Holy Spirit, God, for ever and ever.[1]

These words were etched into my memory from the days when I started to be an altar-server because the local priest used this prayer before every celebration of the Eucharist in the vestry before we walked into church. We never questioned his judgement. He was the customary celebrant. It was the prayer that he was used to saying. And over the years we grew to own it as our preparation for the Eucharist. There were three particular features about the prayer that increasingly struck me as time went on.

First of all, the prayer is addressed to Christ. This gave me little cause to ponder at first. The more normal tradition of liturgical prayer addresses the Father, through the Son, in the Holy Spirit – a convention which the new liturgies have all strengthened. But there has always been another approach which has wanted to speak to Christ direct. When such prayers are allowed in, side-by-side with prayers to the Father, the effect in devotional terms is usually to heighten the personal, intimate dimension. To put it at its most stark, the quiet voice of our celebrant in company with one or two altar-servers reciting this prayer made us feel that we were speaking to Jesus, before we proceeded to celebrate his holy communion.

Then there are two aspects of the prayer itself, two phrases, which kept surfacing in my mind when I heard them said and between times when I pondered them. One was the expression 'memorial of thy passion'. Looking back, I think that they probably formed my understanding of the Eucharist in doctrinal terms more powerfully than almost any other terminology. The meaning of the expression, of course, is open to wide interpretation! But to link the Eucharist with the cross is a fundamental truth which goes right back to Scripture. As Paul writes to the Corinthians, 'For as often as you eat this bread and drink the cup, you proclaim the Lord's death until he comes' (1 Cor. 11:26).

The other part which has kept surfacing over the years is 'perceive within ourselves the fruit of thy redemption'. Surely here is a bold aspiration for the Eucharist. And yet it strikes a supremely Christian note. We can never measure grace in the same way that we can work out the length of a piece of carpet or a person's age or the size of a cake. Nevertheless, if God takes the world seriously and provides us with the means whereby he can reveal himself to us; and if these include the sacraments, more particularly baptism and Eucharist, then we are at least allowed to think that we can be led to expect that God will be at work in us in such a way that we can, just now and then, see some results! Of course, these results need to be kept in contrast to a world that looks for instant results in other directions. But the eucharistic life is about perceiving the fruit of God's redemption and these can be found, for example, in the fruit of the Spirit listed by Paul in his letter to the Galatians, namely 'love, joy, peace, patience, kindness, goodness, faithfulness, gentleness, self-control' (Gal. 5:22).

It is, then, a collect about the Eucharist, and it was originally written for the feast of Corpus Christi, and the evidence points to Thomas Aquinas (*c.* 1225–74) as the author.

WHO WAS THOMAS AQUINAS?[2]

Thomas was born at Roccasecca Castle near Aquino, half-way between Naples and Rome. At the age of five he was sent to the Benedictine school at Monte Cassino. Contrary to his parents' wishes, the brilliant young man decided not to join the Benedictine Order, but instead the comparatively new Order of Preachers, commonly called Dominicans after their founder St Dominic. His parents prevented him from going to Paris, where he could learn more of the new philosophy pioneered in the previous century by Peter Lombard, whose work he read in his enforced captivity.

He eventually got his way and proceeded to Paris, and from there to Cologne, where he was taught by Albert the Great, who described Thomas as 'the dumb ox of Sicily', and who went on to declare that 'this ox will one day fill the world with his bellowing'. In 1252, Thomas went to Paris and lectured on the Bible and the work of Lombard himself. At the time the mendicant Orders were suspect, so that his licence to teach was a tribute to his personal reputation, enhanced by his appointment as regent of the Order. But he became a controversial figure, thanks to hostility from the secular canons, including those of the Abbey of St Victor, and from the other mendicant Order, the Franciscans.

In 1259 he was encouraged to move to Italy, where Pope Urban IV asked him to write the prayers and chants for the new festival of Corpus Christi in 1264. This ensured that the form and style of the language used would be precise and measured. Thomas' skill with words was well known. And his relationship with the Pope was an important one, for he preached on the Eucharist to the Curia on Maundy Thursday that year. He returned to Paris in 1269 for a further tenure of the regency. He was back in Italy in 1272, at Naples, preaching and teaching and writing. He was called to the Council of Lyon, which was intended to heal the rifts between the Eastern and Western Churches. But on his way there he died at Fossanova on 7 March 1274.

Thomas was a prolific writer. He wrote his own commentaries on the works of Peter Lombard, and many treatises, including the *Catena Aurea* ('golden chain'). But he is best known for his *Summa Theologica* ('sum of theology') in the course of which he deals with everything that he could possibly find of importance to belief and the life of faith. It has an energetic rigour and clarity that draws admiration even from detractors. Issues are listed, questions are raised in detail, and answered with even greater detail. We are far away from the careful firmness of

Alcuin, or the passionate concerns of Augustine – though there is more than a little of Augustine's own clarity in Thomas' works.

But apart from the scope of his writing, his approach was new and something of a contrast to Augustine. At the risk of oversimplifying, Augustine and Thomas represent two different approaches which can be traced back to the two ancient Greek philosophers, Plato and Aristotle. We have already seen how Augustine's attitude to the quest for truth is about the present world in relation to a higher world, where the true meaning of things is revealed. What we can see in this world are inadequate copies of the unseen world of ultimate reality. Thomas, on the other hand, adopts the opposite approach, which takes as a basic premise that the external things of this world can help us know God. This was the vital clue, for Thomas, like Albert the Great, his mentor at Cologne, saw the rising fashion of Aristotelian philosophy as posing a challenge to belief in God. It was necessary for them therefore to use the categories of this philosophy not just to explain Christianity in fresh terms but to embellish the new tradition of thinking. Theology has always walked this path and history is full of examples. It is bound to cause tension, not least when there is an established school of thought which perhaps stands in need of adjustment or challenge. As far as the Eucharist is concerned, the kind of language used to describe its meaning focuses on the two Aristotelian concepts of 'substance' (what a thing is in itself) and 'accident' (its outward form). Thomas used these terms in his theological approach to the Eucharist. But before we proceed, we must take a look at what gave rise to his writings as these focus on the feast of Corpus Christi.

THE FEAST OF CORPUS CHRISTI: BACKGROUND[3]

The Eucharist suffers from – or enjoys – an innate capacity to adapt itself to any environment. By the thirteenth century, the majority of celebrations of mass took place at side-altars and were recited silently by a priest, assisted by a server, with or without a congregation. Across the centuries, the Eucharist had known principally two other environments. In the early centuries, the community have often gathered in an adapted house-church for worship and instruction, and to conduct its affairs in a corporate fashion. From the clues that can be picked up from

Augustine's writings, something of this atmosphere lingered into his time, with a lot of talking before the start of the service, a point which was marked only by Augustine himself calling the assembly to order. From the fourth century onwards, however, as Christianity gradually became the public established religion, the Eucharist moved into the larger and more formal environment of the 'basilicas', such as San Clemente in Rome. Here there could be processions, more attention was paid to liturgical chant, and a group of different ministries were expressed in the offering of the service itself, with lessons read by subdeacons and deacons, and the sermon usually given from a pulpit-like desk, because to preach from the chair behind the altar (as before) was not sufficient for visiblity or audibility.

When exactly the side-altar mass developed is hard to tell, but we can see it already growing in the kind of provision we saw in Alcuin of York's list of mass-prayers for different occasions and needs. In many of the older liturgies, particularly in the East, the intercessions still begin with the words, 'we offer for such-and-such'. It was a recognisable short-hand and meant that the whole Eucharist was being celebrated remembering the needs of the world. But the question of balance rears its head. It is one thing to interpret this kind of offering in those general, pastoral terms. It is another to regard the Eucharist as having the power to do something functional on behalf of what it is offered for. And this was one of the Reformers' objections in the sixteenth century.

By the thirteenth century, receiving communion had for most people declined to a few times a year. In 1215 the Fourth Lateran Council enjoined private confession as a prerequisite for receiving communion in any case. The chalice was gradually withheld from the laity. We now have a somewhat different scenario of eucharistic celebration from previous centuries. The list of Alcuin masses, which was already considerably increased by others elsewhere in his own lifetime with many more specific 'votive' forms, helped to underscore an approach to the Eucharist done by the priest on behalf of others. Devotionally strong, the mass was nonetheless weak on participation – the reverse of many Eucharists today. But it was not just liturgical practice that was developing. Eucharistic theology had long been debated. In the ninth century, the two basic approaches to eucharistic presence, which we may generally refer to as 'realist' and 'spiritual', surfaced in the writings of Paschasius Radbertus (*c.* 790–865) and Ratramnus (d. 868), and a similar controversy took place in the eleventh century between Lanfranc (*c.* 1010–89) and Berengar of Tours (*c.* 1010–88). In both these particular controversies, the Catholic Church's instinct was always to opt for the 'realist' position, a harbinger of what was to happen at the Reformation.

What Corpus Christi does, effectively, is to enshrine that 'realist' position at a time when the Eucharist had a life that was light-years away from all that is admired in the Western churches of today. But it must not distract us from that life and that world, for the call for this festival came not from theologians or ecclesiastics. As is so often the case, it came from the 'consumers' themselves, in this case, from a devotional tradition that cried out for a special focus on the presence of Christ adored and loved, and prayed for and prayed to. Juliana of Mont-Cornillon, near Liège, was a nun who had a vision in which the Church was a moon with a dark spot – which represented the absence of a festival of the Lord's body. As we shall see when we look at Gertrude the Great, the role of the nun became significant in the life of the Church in the thirteenth century. If that was how some people felt, then a feast of the Eucharist seemed inevitable.

EUCHARISTIC THEOLOGY AND CORPUS CHRISTI

At the heart of the feast of Corpus Christi are the three variable mass-prayers, the collect, the prayer over the offerings, and the post-communion. Although scholars are not agreed over whether Thomas wrote them on his own, or whether he might have revised earlier texts drafted by others and used in connection with the feast's local burgeoning in the Low Countries, we may assume that these particular prayers are the work of the Angelic Doctor (as he was later called) himself. Because of their overall approach, they are worth quoting in full in a modern translation:

> Lord, you left us in this wonderful sacrament a memorial of your passion: grant us, we pray, so to venerate the sacred mysteries of your Body and Blood, that we may always find within us the fruit of your redemption.

Lord, we pay you, mercifully grant your Church the gifts of unity and peace which are symbolized in a mystery beneath the gifts which we offer.

Grant us, Lord, to be filled with the everlasting enjoyment of your divinity, which is prefigured by our reception here in time of your precious Body and Blood.[4]

The first point to note about these prayers is that they are conceived as forming a pattern. The collect speaks of the Eucharist as a memorial of the passion, the prayer over the offerings sees the Eucharist as the focus of the Church's unity and peace, while the concluding prayer looks forward to the vision of God in heaven, which the Eucharist prefigures. These are the ways in which past, present and future combine to make the Eucharist what it is, and Bernard Capelle, in an article published some years ago, showed how these prayers correspond with Thomas' writings. The Eucharist is about 'remembering' Christ's passion. It is about building up the unity and peace of the Church as it lives in a divided and troubled world. It is about looking forward through its eucharistic celebration to the glory of heaven itself. Each of these views beckons outwards from where the worshipper is situated. Each has an equal importance, which means that if one or other gets forgotten another takes over and dominates. Some would say that history is rather full of the latter tendency.

In terms of Thomas' own writings, the collect corresponds with his views on the eucharistic memorial as a sacrifice. Thomas devoted less space to this area than he did on how Christ is present in the sacrament.[5] Here is a key passage:

Insofar as it is a sacrifice, it has effect also in others for whom it is offered, in whom it does not need that spiritual life should already exist in fact but only in possibility; and therefore, if it finds them disposed, it obtains grace for them by the power of that real sacrifice, from which all grace has flowed into us, and in consequence it blots out mortal sins in them, not as an immediate cause, but insofar as it obtains for them the grace of contrition.

Here is a careful argument for the uniqueness of the sacrifice of Christ, and the way in which the Eucharist applies its benefits to those who are looking for growth in the life of faith. Although the language is strong, nowhere does it suggest that the Eucharist repeats Calvary.

In terms of Thomas' own writings, the prayer over the offerings corresponds to the presence of Christ. One needs to note that the term 'transubstantiation' does not occur at all! It was not invented by Thomas but by Roland Bandinelli (later Pope Alexander III) in the previous century. What Thomas taught about the presence of Christ is that the substance of the bread after consecration ceases to be bread, because what it is in itself is the body of Christ, whereas the accidents, the outward form, remain those of bread. Here is a typical passage:

> It does not pertain to the body of Christ, insofar as it is a body, nor insofar as it is united to deity, to be in many places; but it has this by reason of consecration and of Transubstantiation, insofar as different pieces of bread, which are transubstantiated into it, are in different places. And because the substance of the bread passes into the body of Christ, the accidents remaining, therefore the quantity of each piece of bread remains, and in consequence the place of each piece of bread.

For Thomas, the substance of anything is always developing into something else, like a human being growing up, or wood turning into ash. Therefore it is not unnatural to regard the eucharistic bread and wine turning, in substance, into something else, for which they were intended. Consecration 'transubstantiates' the bread and wine into the body and blood of Christ, because that is what the Lord intends them to become.

It will be apparent that these two prayers are more reticent about the doctrinal issues than Thomas' own writings. Prayers overloaded with didactic, doctrinal language do not usually last in the repertoire! Worship and tradition are not autonomous from the ways in which thought develops, but worship needs its own creative ambiguity in order to resonate for the worshipper and absorb different ideas, and tradition needs to stand between worship and theology in order to act as a kind of organic buffer. Nevertheless, one can see the relationship between the two – how the prayers express the memorial of the passion and the unity and peace of the Church. One can equally see how Thomas' theology expresses the relationship between the mass and what Christ did on the cross, and the relationship between the search for unity and peace through eating and drinking together. As David Power has recently shown, the strengths are obvious: here is a logical system, which draws together the life of nature and the life of grace. Nature is transubstantiated by grace. The Eucharist can never on these terms become a mental activity and one could never conceive of the possibility of throwing the bread and wine away afterwards if not all has been needed for the communion. Thomas' language exudes a sense of reverence before mystery. It was not coined for the different atmopshere of Reformation combat.

But the weaknesses are also apparent, particularly if Thomas' language is taken too literally and the 'mystery factor' is played down. This is what surfaced at the Reformation, when voices clamoured for a closer connection between the presence of Christ in the bread and wine and *faithful reception* – meaning everyone receiving, in both kinds, as well as being devotionally prepared – and for a clearer distinction between Calvary and Supper. Ironically, the eucharistic prayer which had been used for centuries (the Roman Canon, as it is often called, in effect the first eucharistic prayer in the 1970 Roman Missal) expresses these insights succinctly when it prays: 'Bless and approve our offering: make it acceptable to you, an offering in spirit and in truth. *Let it become for us* the body and blood of Jesus Christ. . .' The 'for us' is significant, for it means the congregation receiving, and it also means a relationship between the gifts and the communicants that does not see the gifts in isolation from them.

But the real surprise for a twentieth-century observer is in that post-communion prayer, with its confidence about the relationship between Eucharist and heaven. This has seldom been an area of controversy, because on the whole people have either taken to the idea or they have ignored it. In his book *Eucharist and Eschatology*, Geoffrey Wainwright has performed a considerable service in alerting us to the rich treasures in the past where this theme has been explored.[6] A rich and well-presented plea for the wider tradition, his work is also a firm protest against seeing the Eucharist in exclusively temporal terms. If we do not not look forward to the end of all things, if we do not look beyond what we can perceive and know now, then our Eucharist becomes stunted in its life and growth.

THE LEGACY OF THOMAS AQUINAS

It is impossible for any Westerner to look seriously at the Eucharist without taking into consideration the work of Thomas Aquinas. The unfortunate aspect is that his language became the target of severe criticism from the other strand of Western theology – the 'spiritualist' tendency, which felt that the 'realist' approach had had the upper hand for too long. This is one version of what the Reformation was about, as it sought to purify tradition and move the Eucharist back into a more obviously corporate environment. But there has always been another tendency, which has sought to nuance tradition, balance it out, and draw together the best in any age.

When Richard Hooker (1554–1600) wrote his *Laws of Ecclesiastical Polity*, he tackled the issue of presence as follows:

> Christ assisting this heavenly banquet with his personal and true presence doth by his own divine power add to the natural substance thereof supernatural efficacy, which addition to the nature of those consecrated elements changeth them and maketh them that unto us which otherwise they could not be; that to us they are thereby made such instruments as mystically yet truly, indivisibly yet really work our communion or fellowship with the person of Jesus Christ, as well in that he is man as God, our participation also in the fruit, grace and efficacy of his body and blood whereupon there ensueth a kind of transubstantiation in us, a true change both of body and soul, an alteration from death to life.[7]

Hooker cannot fail to live in the aftermath of Thomas Aquinas, for he insists that the bread and wine are not what they were but posits any 'transubstantiation' in the faithful communicant. Some might hold that he went too far in the other direction, others would understand the need to redress an important balance. The need for such a balance perhaps arose more from the way in which masses were celebrated in the later Middle Ages (frequently, without communicants apart from the priest) than from the language in which Thomas formulated the 'how' and the 'wherewithal' of the eucharistic bread and wine thus consecrated.

And on sacrifice, Jeremy Taylor (1613–67) adopts another route altogether in a characteristically lush passage:

> [The Eucharist] is the greatest solemnity of prayer, the most power-

a word Newman used.

ful liturgy and means of impetration in this world. For when Christ was consecrated on the cross and became our high priest ... he became infinitely gracious in the eyes of God, and was admitted to the celestial and eternal priesthood in heaven; where in the virtue of the cross. He intercedes for us, and represents an eternal sacrifice in the heavens on our behalf.[8]

In these lines, we can see a similar dynamic at work. Hooker transubstantiates the communicants, Taylor places the sacrifice on the cross. But Hooker asserts that the bread and wine are changed, and Taylor makes the sacrifice eternal by moving it onward from the cross into heaven, and so providing the means whereby the Church can share in that self-offering of love and prayer. It is as if Thomas were being heeded: the bread and wine are not what they were, and the Eucharist is an offering. But the faithful receiver, in the Reformed tradition a mandatory character at every Eucharist, shares in this change, and partakes in the One Offering. And yet, if one looks again at what Thomas wrote, the distance is not so great after all. As with the great truths of Christianity, we are faced with the need to live with paradox.

Thomas Aquinas' liturgical work included a number of rich hymns, as well as the following poem which is attributed to him and which has entered the repertoire of eucharistic hymnody in various translations. James Woodford (1820–85), Bishop of Ely, translated its main stanzas, which begin:

> Thee we adore, O hidden Saviour, thee,
> Who in thy Sacrament dost deign to be:
> Both flesh and spirit at thy Presence fail,
> Yet here thy Presence we devoutly hail.[9]

I have sung this hymn on many occasions. One in particular stands out prominently. I attended the Eucharist at the beginning of the academic year in October 1966 for the Faculty of Divinity at Edinburgh University in St Giles' Cathedral. The rite was that of the (Presbyterian) Church of Scotland. As the elders processed in with the bread and wine, these thirteenth-century aspirations echoed round an ecumenical congregation in a medieval edifice. The final verse had a particular poignancy in the light of all the eucharistic controversies that have raged in the period since:

Why do Anglicans always have to add this word: it is The Church of Scotland!

> O Christ, whom now beneath a veil we see,
> May what we thirst for soon our portion be:
> To gaze on thee unveiled, and see thy face,
> The vision of thy glory and thy grace.

Gertrude the Great

THE WOUNDS PRAYER

Lord Jesus Christ, Son of the living God, grant that I may aspire to you with all my heart, with abundant desire, with thirsting soul. Grant that I may respire in you, who are most sweet and most delightful. Grant that my whole spirit and all my inner being may unceasingly pant after you who are true blessedness. Most merciful Lord, write your wounds in my heart with your precious blood, that I may read in them your suffering and your love alike. Then may the mindfulness of your wounds remain with me unceasingly in the recesses of my heart, that sorrow for your suffering may be aroused in me and the ardour of your love may be enkindled in me. Grant also that all creation may grow worthless in my eyes, and that you alone may impart sweetness to my heart.[10]

Since 1980, Guildford and Freiburg-im-Breisgau have enjoyed a cordial 'twinning' and there are many areas of the lives of both places that have benefited greatly from the interchanges that take place from time to time. At the civic level the relationships are close and when a delegation from Freiburg was coming to Guildford in March 1995, I was approached by the Chief Executive – a Roman Catholic – to see whether the official parties could attend the Sung Eucharist in Holy Trinity on the Sunday morning. There was no problem about such a request and we accordingly set to work to ensure that the service matched the occasion. There would be a special service-sheet with the main parts of the liturgy – and, where appropriate, the hymns – in both English and German. To cap it all, the organist played in conclusion a transcripton of Wagner's *Meistersinger* overture.

The reason for the visit was to make a 'return gesture' after the Mayor of Guildford's trip to Freiburg in the previous November to commemorate the fiftieth anniversary of the bombing of the old German city in 1944. It was important that our Eucharist should not be bland (on the one hand) or confrontational (on the other). The sermon, preached by a colleague, centred on how God always starts with us as we are and how the unforgiven figure prominently on the terrain of his grace. Near the start of the liturgy would come the confession. How could that be introduced appropriately?

For some time I had been reading *The Herald of God's Loving-Kindness* by Gertrude the Great, who was a German mystic who lived in the thirteenth century. One of the main features of her writings is her devotion to the heart and the wounds of Christ. When musing on these divine truths on one occasion, she herself came across the prayer quoted above, and it helped her to develop her thought. After a long phone-call with a friend who speaks German fluently, part of this prayer was translated into that language and I read it out in both English and German before we said the confession at the Eucharist the next day. The whole service made a deep impression both on our visitors and the regular congregation. Particularly eloquent was that part of the prayer which asked God to 'write your wounds in my heart with your precious blood.' But with those wounds come also the beating human heart, 'aspiring', 'respiring', 'panting', in its 'recesses'. We are back to Augustine again. Although the prayer was (apparently) written originally in Latin, my translator quickly suggested that it fell so naturally into German (*schreibe Deine Wunden mit Deinem kostbaren Blut in meine Seele*) as to indicate original composition in the vernacular.[11] The answer to that riddle, however, may have to wait a long time before being finally resolved.

GERTRUDE THE GREAT: HER LIFE AND WORK[12]

Gertrude was born in 1256 probably near Helfta which is south-east of Eisleben near Halle. As one looks back on her life and the conditions through which her community lived, it really is remarkable that she made enough impact to be called 'the Great' within a few centuries of her death. She was presented to a community of nuns at the age of five, perhaps because she was orphaned or possibly because of a stepmother who did not like her. The nuns at Helfta were a new community founded in 1258 and it is not clear whether they were Benedictine or they belonged to the new (stricter) Cistercian observance. From what we know they were more Cistercian in their lifestyle than Benedictine. She was frequently ill. And after her death the convent

was destroyed by Albert of Brunswick in 1342, though the community was reinstated at Eisleben four years later as a
'New Helfta'. She herself died on 7 November 1301 (possibly
1302).

In her writings she shows a high level of theological knowledge. Nuns were not educated in the new learning of the
schools, which means that Peter Lombard and Thomas Aquinas
were closed books to her. But she was well-versed in the Fathers
and she makes frequent use of Augustine and Gregory the Great,
among others. In character she was lively and humorous. She
liked liturgical chant. She worked as a copyist in the 'scrip-
torium', the medieval equivalent of the photocopying-room –
though doubtless more decorous. *The Herald* is a collection of
observations on many aspects of the spiritual life in four books,
the first of which is a kind of biography written by another nun.
It is probably only Book 2 – a series of revelations and thoughts
dated 1289–90 – which is through-and-through Gertrude herself. But there is enough to go on from that. Augustine's influence is strong and there are allusions to the *Confessions* in several
places.

There are two features of her work which stand out as being
of particular interest, apart from the fact that it is strongly
liturgical (she frequently refers to the Offices, their hymns and
prayers), eucharistic (she has a deep devotion to receiving the
sacrament frequently) and Trinitarian (she is constantly praying
to God in all three persons).

First of all she writes with a great deal of feeling – even of
passion. There is nothing of the clipped logician about her. One
Christmas at midnight mass, she describes herself as 'collecting
myself somewhat to fondle you with loving caresses'. This passion is reflected in the way she speaks of 'returning to my heart'
in an echo of one of the passages from Augustine's *Confessions*
which we looked at earlier. But it spills over into her description
of vivid experiences of the presence of Christ in the beatific
vision:

> When you had brought me, quite undeserving, up against that most
> desirable face which was manifesting the treasures of all blessedness
> ... I felt light entering through my own eyes, a light which came
> from your deifying eyes, a light beyond price, bringer of sweetness,

which penetrated all my inner being and seemed to produce an extraordinarily supernatural effect in all my limbs.[13]

Secondly, Gertrude's piety takes her to the wounds of Christ, as the prayer quoted earlier indicates. In the passage which follows this in *The Herald* we find the following account:

At the time I mentioned, when my mind was occupied with the subject with great devotion, I became aware that what I had just sought in the prayer I mentioned had been conferred on me, as if by divine intervention, utterly unworthy as I was. Inwardly in my heart, as if in physical places, I realized the Spirit had impressed the worshipful and adorable imprint of your most holy wounds. By those wounds you healed my soul and gave me the cup of the nectar of love to drink.[14]

We have a great deal here. The passage is an address to Christ but the Holy Spirit is the means whereby the wounds have been impressed on her. The experience recounted is a total cleansing, a renewal, as if baptism were being renewed and healing imparted. And it is a powerful experience – hence the reference to 'divine intervention'.

Gertrude was writing at a time when the wounds of Christ were slowly making their way into popular piety. A mass of the Five Wounds of Christ begins to make its appearance around this time and in this area. Its collect is worth quoting in full:

O Lord Jesus Christ, you came down to earth from the bosom of your Father in heaven, and shed your precious blood for the remission of our sins; we humbly entreat you that on the day of judgement, standing at your right hand, we may be found worthy to hear those words: Come, blessed ones; You, who are God living and reigning with the same God the Father and the Holy Spirit.[15]

It is not hard to place Gertrude's account and this collect side-by-side and see a correspondence between the affective piety of the mystic and the liturgical prose of the Church. Moreover, Julian of Norwich describes a more graphic experience in *Revelations of Divine Love*.[16] Like Thomas Aquinas' Corpus Christi collect, that for the mass of the Five Wounds is also addressed to Christ direct, thus heightening the ambience conveyed by the imagery. The mystical experience and the collect underline a significant aspect of the development of tradition, not unlike the emergence of the feast of Corpus Christi itself: piety and liturgy and theology need to have a continued dialogue with each other. If piety disappears into a world of its own, public worship becomes arid and theology is deprived of the opportunity to fulfil its most basic function, which is to prevent religion degenerating into superstition.

The major difference, however, between the experience as recounted and the collect is that the experience is described as a breaking into history of eternity, whereas the collect projects the imagery into heaven itself, with the 'bosom of the Father' inaugurating Christ's ministry and the Father's right hand as the place where judgement will be given (Matt. 25:31–46). But both Gertrude's account and the prayer describe *movement* – in both cases initiated by God and in both cases desired by humanity.

From the devotion to the Wounds of Christ came, too, the Sacred Heart. Their outward and liturgical features were set aside at the Reformation, which included the curious custom of inserting 'incense grains' (not identified with the five wounds until the late thirteenth century) in the Paschal Candle at the Easter Vigil.[17] But the wounds and heart of Christ were too powerful as ways of depicting the sacred humanity of Christ for them to remain in devotional exile for long. Puritans like Richard Baxter (1615–91) found its allusions to the spiritual aspects of the piercing of Christ's side by the spear (John 19:34ff) a welcome inspiration for piety.[18] Like the Aquinas eucharistic poem-hymn quoted earlier, this strand of spirituality survived into modern hymnody. When the first edition of *Hymns Ancient and Modern* was published in 1861, Sir Henry Baker, one of the leading lights of the hymnal committee, produced a translation of a hymn which appeared in Latin in a Roman Catholic book in Cologne in 1695. I cannot sing it without hearing ringing in my ears the words of Gertrude the Great, testimony to women's memory in every age, of the Spirit impressing 'the worshipful and adorable imprint of your most holy wounds':

> Jesu, grant me this, I pray,
> Ever in my heart to stay;
> Let me evermore abide
> Hidden in thy wounded side.

If the world or Satan lay
Tempting snares about my way,
I am safe when I abide
In thy heart and wounded side.

If the flesh, more dangerous still,
Tempt my soul to deeds of ill,
Naught I fear when I abide
In thy heart and wounded side.

Death will come one day to me;
Jesu, cast me not from thee:
Dying let me still abide
In thy heart and wounded side.[19]

*Charles Wesley came in later
a five bleeding wounds to be
Received on Calvary . . . .
& Jervaul/Maaurron this.*

CHAPTER FIVE

Lancelot Andrewes: Preacher Extraordinary

A MEMORIAL IN WINCHESTER CATHEDRAL

> You thought you should have come to Christ's resurrection today, and so you do. But not to his alone, but even to Mary Magdalene's resurrection, too. For, in very deed, a kind of resurrection it was, was wrought in her; revived, as it were, and raised from a dead and drooping, to a lively and cheerful estate. The gardener had done his part, made her all green on the sudden.[1]

Saturday 1 February 1995 was a memorable occasion in the life of Winchester Cathedral, for at Evensong a memorial to Lancelot Andrewes was dedicated by his twentieth-century successor. It had long been felt that such a memorial was overdue. After all, Andrewes was probably one of the most distinguished holders of that office in recent centuries. The day itself grew 'like Topsy'. In the morning, an informal seminar took place under the leadership of David Scott, Director of the School of Spirituality in the diocese, and himself an Andrewes enthusiast. After lunch, a public lecture was given in St Swithun's Church by Nicholas Lossky, a Russian Orthodox lay theologian from Paris, himself a considerable authority on Andrewes. Finally, at Evensong the choir of the Cathedral was filled to overflowing with a congregation gathered from many institutions with whom Andrewes had a connection. These included the Merchant Taylors' School (where Andrewes was a pupil), Pembroke College Cambridge (where he studied and was a Fellow), Westminster Abbey (where he was Dean), and Southwark Cathedral (where he was buried); and the Bishops of Chichester and Ely – where Andrewes was bishop before going on to Winchester – attended as well.

The memorial was made by Simon Verity, one of the finest

stone-carvers in the country, and at the time engaged in an ambitious programme of carving on the Cathedral of St John the Divine, New York. The surround is made of grey lias, from the West Country, on which are carved various symbols of Andrewes' interests. The centrepiece is of Italian marble and has a series of inscriptions with Andrewes' dates, a quotation from one of his prayers, and the bold description, 'Bishop, Pastor, Man of God'. Above the centrepiece is a bust of Andrewes, based on the portraits available, and this is in Alabama marble. And no Bishop of Winchester can fail to take notice of the man, for the memorial is situated immediately to the east of the bishop's throne in the choir.

Memorials of this kind have their personal touches. The Andrewes memory lives on in the people who worship in the Cathedral. Both the Bishop, Colin James, and the Dean, Trevor Beeson, were men in whom history forms a strong life-force. They were keen that it should be erected. As the choir sang Vittoria's 'O quam gloriosum est regnum' (= 'O how glorious is the kingdom') the bishops and clergy gathered round the memorial. As a fitting prelude to its dedication, Colin James read from Andrewes' sermons – an extract from the one quoted above. It was preached by Andrewes as Bishop of Winchester on Easter Day 1620 before King James I in Whitehall. In many ways a typical Andrewes nugget, it shines out with his own peculiar combination of Easter as the foundation of Christian living and human experience. Jesus is, after all, the gardener. There is no mistake, for he gardens those who seek him. 'The gardener had done his part, made her all green on the sudden.'

After the blessing of the memorial, two of Andrewes' prayers were offered, and the service concluded with one of Charles Wesley's most eloquent hymns on the Trinity, 'Father, in whom we live/ In whom we are, and move'. Wesley drank deeply of Andrewes' sermons. The hymn in question invokes the three persons of the Trinity and creates a wonderful scene of the saints singing the praises of God for ever. History is full of ironies. Why should it take nearly 370 years before such a memorial finds itself in Winchester Cathedral? In one sense, it does not really matter. It is there, after all! But perhaps it is a small witness to the recovery today of a wider and deeper sense of tradition in Andrewes' own church at least.

BISHOP, PASTOR, MAN OF GOD

From his earliest days, it seems, Andrewes had all the markings of a studious and contemplative character.[2] He took to academic work so enthusiastically that, apparently, his parents had to make him play when he was a boy. Apart from his achievements as a prominent cleric, his life spanned a time of considerable change in English life. Born in 1555, he was an infant at the end of the reign of Mary Tudor and grew up to manhood and the main part of his career under Queen Elizabeth I. At her death, there being no Tudor heir, King James VI of Scotland came south and became James I of England. By the time he died in 1626, Charles I was on the throne, and Andrewes is even credited with foreseeing a troubled reign for the incoming monarch when he was heir apparent to the throne. For someone like Andrewes living in England through these years, there must have been a strong awareness of change and instability in many different aspects of society.

Andrewes' father was a merchant seaman, and although he never travelled abroad, it was probably from him that he inherited a love of languages and a sense of being part of a much larger world than the one in which day-to-day business was transacted. At Cambridge, Andrewes was clearly aware of the rising tide of Puritan attitudes, which would try to move the Church of England in a more Protestant direction. Those in power identified Andrewes as a man of great ability. He not only taught at Cambridge but he preached as well, an activity which was obviously important to him. In 1589, he was appointed to the parish of St Giles', Cripplegate, in the city of London, and given a canon's stall in St Paul's Cathedral. By tradition, that particular stall had attached to it the role of penitentiary – spiritual direction and hearing confessions. Andrewes took this side of things seriously and walked up and down St Paul's Cathedral at appointed times in order to be available to people for advice and spiritual counsel. Not many people availed themselves of this ministry – popular prejudice was against it – but some people did, and from that kind of contact Andrewes built up a reputation as a wise pastor. Indeed, he preached a powerful – and controversial – sermon on absolution on the First Sunday after Easter in 1600.[3]

It was common for able priests to have more than one post

and in 1597 Andrewes was appointed to a canonry in Westminster Abbey. Although the junior member of chapter, he nonetheless succeeded to the deanery in 1601, which placed him in a prominent position when King James arrived in London and was crowned. The two developed a close relationship, which is spelt out in the directions for James' coronation. Andrewes prepared him spiritually for the solemn occasion and walked on his right-hand all through the service, even though the King was supported by two bishops. At the communion, the Archbishop of Canterbury administered the consecrated bread to the King, but it was Andrewes who administered the chalice. Hitherto, the rite had been in Latin, and the Eucharist according to Roman Catholic procedures. Andrewes, it would seem, played an important part in drawing up what was the first fully Protestant coronation service in English history.

King James wanted Andrewes made a bishop and this took place in 1606, when he went to Chichester, from where he proceeded to Ely in 1609, finally moving to Winchester in 1619. As a bishop, Andrewes preached frequently at the main festivals before the King, either at Whitehall or else in the place where the court was residing at the time. So important was Andrewes to the King that many people expected him to be appointed to Canterbury in 1611, but instead George Abbot, Bishop of London, became the new Archbishop. Andrewes may have had his enemies at court. Abbot certainly had his champion, the Earl of Dunbar. In any event, Andrewes was able to exert his influence on national affairs through the oblique medium of being a regular court preacher over a period of 20 years.

THE *PRIVATE PRAYERS*

A man's death often sums up his whole life. Andrewes was a man of books, but the only book he wanted near him in his last days was his own collection of private prayers, which were written in Latin, Greek, and (where the source required it) in Hebrew. This book of prayers was never intended for publication but it has been printed and translated into English on several occasions since. There were a number of versions in circulation in the years following his death, and yet one more has turned up in a recent acquisition in Lambeth Palace Library.

Usually referred to as the *Preces Privatae* – or *Private Prayers*

– they provide a window into Andrewes' soul. Carefully laid out on the page, they give the appearance of having been written in blank verse, for slow recitation and meditation. There are prayers for each day of the week, there are eucharistic devotions, and there are extended meditations on the Lord's Prayer. Fundamental to Andrewes' piety, however, is the creed. There are several prayers which give the appearance of having been inspired by the sheer fact of belief, the corporate faith of the Church applied to the individual soul. Here is one example, in a fresh translation:

> I believe that you created me:
>   let not the work of your hands be despised.
> I believe that I am after your image and likeness:
>   let not your own likeness be defaced.
> I believe that you saved me by your blood:
>   let not the price of the ransom be squandered.
> I believe that you proclaimed me a Christian in your name:
>   let not your namesake be scorned.
> I believe that you hallowed me in rebirth:
>   let not that consecration be despoiled.
> I believe that you engrafted me into the cultivated olive-tree:
>   let not the limb of your mystical body be cut out.[4]

In 1903, F. E. Brightman produced an edition of the *Private Prayers* with a detailed list of sources. More significant still, he included a series of quotations from Andrewes' sermons that echo the prayers. Yet more striking is the fact that in this particular case, all the echoes come from the same sermon, one of a series on the Lord's Prayer:

> We are thy workmanship created by Thee; therefore 'despise not the works of thy own hands.'

> Besides, we are the 'likeness' of God's image; therefore suffer not thine own image to be defaced in us, but repair it.

> Secondly, in regard of Christ, we are the price of Christ's blood. *Empti estis pretio*, 'Ye are bought with a price'; therefore suffer not so great a price to be lost, but deliver and save us.

> Again, we carry his name, for as He is Christ, so we are of Him called Christians. Seeing, therefore, that 'thy name is called upon us,' be gracious to us and grant our request.

From these references, it is not hard to detect a direct correspondence between what the man preached and what he prayed. Numerous other examples could be given. This instance is all the more intriguing because each of the four quotations from the sermon come from the very same page. More important, however, is the onward drive of the prayer itself. We are created in God's image and likeness, we are saved by redemption in Christ, we are claimed as his own, we are baptised through the waters of rebirth, and we are part of the eucharistic community, the Church. And yet there is no cheap triumphalism in the prayer. Each statement is followed by a prayer. The statement is tinged with hope. The prayer evokes both penitence and confidence. And between the lines one can read the Trinity of persons, creating, redeeming and sustaining not only a particular individual, but a community, indeed a whole environment. It is a supremely *Christian* prayer.

THE SERMONS

When Andrewes died, Charles I charged two senior bishops, William Laud of London, and John Buckeridge of Rochester (later of Ely) to draw together a collection of Andrewes' sermons for publication. It did not take them long, and in 1629, the '96' sermons made their first appearance in published form. Since that date, they have been reprinted several times, firstly in the ensuing years (I have in my possession a copy of one of the early editions), and then more recently in 1842. In our own time, Marianne Dorman has published selected highlights from them, and P. E. Hewson has put together a selection which includes the full text of six sermons, extracts from three others (all Christmas preachings), together with some extracts from the *Private Prayers*.[5]

Laud and Buckeridge, who had preached at Andrewes' funeral, dedicate the book to King Charles I with the following words which explain the nature and purpose of the venture:

> We here present to your most sacred majesty a book of sermons. We need not tell whose they are, the sermons are able to speak their author. When the author died, your majesty thought it not fit his sermons should die with him. And though they could not live with all that elegancy which they had upon his tongue, yet you were

graciously pleased to think a paper-life better than none. Upon this your majesty gave us a strict charge, that we should overlook [= look over] the papers [as well sermons as other treatises] of that reverend and worthy prelate, and print all that we found perfect. There came to our hands a world of sermon-notes, but these came perfect. Had they not come perfect, we should not have ventured to add any line unto them, lest mixing a pen far inferior, we should have disfigured such complete bodies.

Sermons read after they are preached, whether a few days or months or centuries, are not the same medium as when originally delivered. And the distance of time happily provides a gap between our own age and the particular political agenda with which Laud and King Charles I are associated. From what we know of Andrewes, he was a man of more moderate political style, devoted as he was to the monarchy. As is often the case, a preacher who is popular in one age will go out of fashion in another. We know that Andrewes' approach, imitated as it was by others, was considered old-fashioned and insufficiently practical at the time of the Restoration in 1660. But the fact that the '96' are still being looked at and sifted and studied so many years on marks out Andrewes as a truly remarkable and universal figure. In making their choice, the two editors decided to include the main sermons preached at court at Christmas, Lent, Easter, Whitsunday, and also a number of other sermons given on such occasions as 5 November (the 'Gunpowder' day). At the end of the collection are 11 miscellaneous sermons which stand out on their own.

In our own century, Andrewes has experienced something of a mild revival, thanks in part to T. S. Eliot who wrote an essay about him in 1928. He covers a number of features. Andrewes needs to be read carefully. His style is at times a strange mixture of the long, complex sentence and the direct, lively image. He has a mind that sees things whole and can draw into his journey any amount of biblical allusion or quotation from ancient authors. And, above all, he has a definite structure, which helps the reader along. But Eliot's defining quality, it seems to me, in describing Andrewes is as follows: 'Andrewes' emotion is purely contemplative; it is not personal, it is wholly evoked by the object of contemplation, to which it is adequate; his emotion is wholly contained in and explained by its object.'[6]

Not many have commented on Andrewes' 'emotion' but it is there. And those who wrote about him remember his speed and liveliness of delivery. I would add a further quality – humour. There is a warmth of humanity in his preaching that can easily be forgotten simply because one is looking at a dusty tome printed in a bygone age. The congregations at the court services would include not only the great and the good, they would also include the servants. Andrewes knew how to lodge an idea in people's minds. In those days, it was standard for those who had a formal education to learn to remember discourses by thinking of an empty room into which one placed furniture as part of the process of remembering. But for each one who had this advantage, there would be others who lacked it and it was probably for their benefit that Andrewes flung himself into such sentiments as: 'A cold coming they had of it, at this time of the year; just the worst time of the year, to take a journey, and specially a long journey, in.' This comes from Andrewes' 1622 Christmas sermon, which inspired Eliot's poem, 'Journey of the Magi', even down to Andrewes' mannerism, 'set down this.'[7]

More recently, Nicholas Lossky has published a study of Andrewes' sermons from a theological point of view. He captures in a flash how Andrewes approaches the things of God when he wants to speak of them to others, or pray to God about them on his own: 'It is someone for whom theology is not a system of thought, an intellectual construction, but a progression in the experience of the mystery, the way of union with God in the communion of the Church.'[8]

We have so far sipped some of his preaching and praying, and have seen them in the context of his age. Now is the time to look more closely at three of his sermons. We have chosen them for the different ways in which the Scripture texts are handled. In Christmas 1619, Andrewes squeezes as much as he can from the song of the angels (Luke 2:14). In Easter 1620, he takes us through every dramatic stage of the scene of Mary Magdalene in the garden (John 20:11–17). And in Whitsun 1617, he applies Jesus' text in the synagogue at Nazareth (Luke 4:18–19) to the festival and to the Church.

Christmas 1619[9]

Andrewes preached this sermon on Christmas Day at Whitehall
on the song of the angels (Luke 2:14). It was his first sermon as
Bishop of Winchester. Reading it, one gets the impression of
someone enjoying himself as he goes over and over again a text
whose words will have been very familiar. 'Glory be to God on
high. . .' are not only the opening words of the angel-hymn in
Luke's narrative of Christ's birth. They also begin the ancient
hymn of the Church, which in Andrewes' day came at the end
of the Eucharist. One can imagine a few of his hearers thinking,
as he began, 'What on earth is he going to make of this?'

From the very start, it is clear that Andrewes wants his hearers
to consider that they are taking part in this song *now*:

> That heaven and earth, and men are to join in one consort: heaven
> and earth first; heaven on high, earth beneath to take up one hymn:
> both in honour of his birth, both are better by it; heaven hath glory,
> earth peace by means of it. Heaven hath glory; earth, peace; at thy
> nativity, O Lord. Warranted by this song; at thy nativity, O Lord,
> let the heavens rejoice for the glory: let the earth be glad for the
> peace, that come to them by it.

We are left in no doubt that Andrewes is about to give us a
series of sparkling thoughts on the union of earth and heaven,
and the way in which glory from heaven effects peace on earth.
And he suggests, following early writers, that in glory, peace and
goodwill are to be found the three persons of the Trinity; Father
in the glory, Christ in peace, and goodwill in the Holy Spirit.

Then Andrewes moves into a discussion of the two versions
of the text as they appear in the liturgical traditions. The Prayer
Book followed the Greek tradition in translating the line in a
logical sequence: glory to God on high, peace on earth, goodwill
towards men. And this helps him to place Christ in the centre
as both God and Man – a neat way of preaching about the
incarnation:

> You will mark: the child (here) is God and Man. God, from on high;
> Man, from the earth. To heaven, whence he is God, thither goeth
> glory: to earth, whence man, thither peace. Then, as God and Man
> is one Christ; and as the reasonable soul and flesh is one man: so,
> Christ consisting of these two brings goodwill, the fulness of God's
> favour, the true and real cause of both; yielding them peace, while

here on earth, and assuring them of glory, when there on high; as thither on high, we trust to be delivered, after our time here spent in procuring heaven glory, and earth peace; thus, three rests.

Andrewes is making music! And the musical analogy provides the opportunity to move into the Latin version of the line, which has two rests – glory to God on high, peace to men on earth of goodwill. Such an understanding has much to commend it: 'either is well; but both and best: for both are most true.'

As if this were not enough, we are then told that there is no verb, so is it a declaration or is it a wish? Andrewes expands on both possibilities:

Many favours, much goodwill before; never so, as when God and Man, the Godhead and Manhood meet both in one. God never so pleased, as when he was pleased to assume it, into one person with himself, uniting both with the straightest union that can be.

It is, surely, from this passage that Charles Wesley, in the hymn known today as 'Hark! the herald angels sing', coined the words:

Pleased as Man with Man to dwell,
Jesus our Emmanuel.

But Andrewes prefers the hymn as a wish, for it strikes the right balance between time and eternity, God's time beyond ours, and ours in its limits and its opportunities:

For the work of the day, to make the day of the work a glorious day: causing it to be attended with a number of days, according to the number of the months of the year; as no feast itself. Glorious in all places, as well at home with carols, as in the Church with anthems: glorious in all ages; even this day, this year, as on the very day, on which he was born. Glorious in habit, in fare: but specially (as we see the angels here do) with the service of God, the most solemn service, the highest, the most melodious hymns, we have: and namely, with this here of the choir of heaven.

Which leads him to go on:

And good reason, we should so wish: Christ lost his glory, by being thus in the cratch [= crib]. We took some from him: to wish him some for it again.

Another echo of Charles Wesley, from the same hymn:

Mild he lays his glory by.

Pushing the unity of heaven and earth yet further, he affirms:

> If we sing glory without peace, we sing but to halves. No glory on
> high will be admitted, without peace on earth.

Preferring in his heart the Greek version, Andrewes then
proceeds to play with glory on high, peace on earth, goodwill
to men. Glory only belongs to God, peace is what the earth
needs, and goodwill is what draws the human race together, in
'the music of heaven'. For there is a kind of heaven on earth
when there is peace.

As in so many of Andrewes' sermons, he ends with a call to
his hearers to come to communion (there was an opportunity
for non-communicants to depart):

> And that we might be in that case, and so sing it, the Church is
> never unprovided, this day, of this means of elevating our minds:
> And it is worth the while, if it were but for that; and there may be
> joy among the angels in heaven, to hear their hymn kept still alive.
> Though, there is another congruity for the sacrament; that great
> mystery of Godliness, which is God manifested in the flesh, might
> not be celebrated without the mystery of his flesh: that, the day, he
> came among us to be partaker of flesh and blood, we also might be
> partakers of the flesh and blood which he took from us, to give
> them us again.

Right at the end, we are taken up into heaven, another favourite
device of Andrewes at the end of his sermons:

> Assuring ourselves that the same goodwill that was able to bring
> the Son of God from heaven to earth, shall have the like power to
> lift up the sons of men from earth to the glory of heaven: there
> with the blessed angels, to sing this glorious hymn eternally.

On reading this, one is reminded of yet one more echo from
that Charles Wesley hymn:

> Born to raise the sons of earth,
> Born to give them second birth.

Easter 1620[10]

Andrewes preached this sermon, again at Whitehall, on Easter
Day, 1620. As we have already noted, this sermon is about Mary

Magdalen in the garden looking for Jesus. Whereas Christmas 1619 played with one single verse, this sermon plays with a detailed scene, and, unusual for Andrewes, the discourse is set out in sections each headed by the verse in question. He likes to quote, or allude to, the early Fathers. But in this case, it is clear that Augustine is a major influence – he appears no fewer than six times. And lest the six main sections built around the six main verses seem to break up the unity of the sermon, Andrewes binds the whole together by spreading no fewer than ten arguments for Mary Magdalen's great love over three parts of his discourse!

He begins on a deceptively simple note by saying that the sermon is about the seeking of Christ dead, and finding him. There is a tenderness that permeates this sermon. In no way is he judging Mary Magdalen. Indeed, at one glorious stage, when discussing Mary's readiness to move Jesus' body near the end, he exclaims: 'Love makes women more than women.' That bold statement is the result of his assertion near the start that: 'We cannot commend her faith; her love, we cannot but commend.'

There are many ways of conveying the flavour of this sermon. Those ten arguments for her love are as good as any:

- 'She stood by the grave.'
- 'A stronger affection fixed her.'
- 'She stood and she wept.'
- 'And as she wept, she stooped, and looked in.'
- 'To seek, is one thing: not to give over seeking, is another.'
- 'Her love and respect was no whit abated, by the scandal of his death.'
- 'Of a sudden looking in now, and seeing two [angels] – a sight able to have amazed any; any, but her. It moves her not at all.'
- 'Neither did their [the angels'] comfortable speech work with her at all.'
- 'Her affections seem so to transport her, as she says no man knows what.'
- 'But love makes women more than women, at least as it makes them have the courage above their strength, far.'

These observations come from a man who never married,

hence their double significance. But the underlying theme of love enables Andrewes to do more than just paint a vivid scene and take us through a drama. For it draws the hearer into the workings of God:

> For, he it is, that by virtue of this morning's act, shall garden our bodies, too; turn all our graves into garden-plots: yea, shall one day turn land and sea, and all into a great garden, and so husband them, as they shall in due time bring forth live bodies, even all our bodies alive again.

In the course of this sermon, he refers to Psalms 16 and 30 as 'Resurrection psalms'. And he cunningly tucks a reference to the Trinity into that sense of the absence of God which is an essential part of the experience of every believer: 'Yea, when Christ and the Holy Ghost, and the favour of God, and all is gone, how soon, how easily are we comforted again for all this?' When Mary finally greets Jesus as 'Rabboni', he remarks: 'Nothing so allures, so draws love to it, as doth love itself.'

Near the end, Andrewes observes that 'in matters of faith the ear goes first, ever, and is of more use, and to be trusted before the eye.' And this gives him the chance to confront those who might value the word more than the sacrament, at which he comments that we should give thanks for both and allow them to work in their own way: 'of both which he makes us partakers, who is the author of both, Jesus Christ the righteous.'

Whitsun 1617[11]

The sermon which Andrewes preached at Whitsun in 1617 is unique in the repertoire because it was delivered outside England. When King James followed what he called his 'salmon-like instinct' and decided to travel north to Scotland for the fiftieth anniversary celebrations of his coronation as James VI of Scotland, he took with him Lancelot Andrewes not only as a prominent cleric but also as the preacher in the chapel royal at Holyrood Palace, Edinburgh, at Whitsun. The royal progress northwards was lengthy and expensive – no doubt one of the reasons for James' ministers being against the journey in the first place. There were ceremonial halts at Lincoln Cathedral, and also at Durham, where, on Easter Day Andrewes preached the sermon.

The chapel royal at Holyrood had not been used for a long time, not since James' departure for the south in 1603. Accordingly, it was fitted out decorously for Prayer Book worship and an organ installed. William Laud, then Dean of Gloucester, and not over-endowed with personal skills, had a row with the organ-builder on arrival, and was sent home earlier than expected for his provocative behaviour among the Scots, not all of whom were set against James' plan to reform the Kirk along episcopal lines.

Into this atmosphere came Andrewes to preach the sermon. Taking as his text the well-known passage from Isaiah read by Jesus in the synagogue at Nazareth, 'The Spirit of the Lord is upon me, because he has anointed me. . .' (Luke 4:18–19 = Isa. 61:1–2), he covers a large area of the way in which God and human beings meet and the gifts of God are shared among all. His Whitsun sermons are the most markedly Trinitarian. Near the beginning – another of his favourite devices – he brings in this area of belief in describing the work of the Spirit:

> These three distinct: the Spirit, from the Lord, whose the Spirit is: the Spirit, that was upon, from him, it was upon. Yet all three in one joint concurrence, to one and the same work, the jubilee of the gospel.

The Spirit, therefore, is no vague feeling, but the power of God – the Spirit of Christ, the Spirit of the Father, the Spirit proceeding from God. That intermeshing of persons, with all its dynamism (he suggests that Christ's anointing affected God as well) cannot fail to affect others and draw them into the divine life. Each person of the Trinity is alive and active in the anointing of Jesus: 'to retain to each person his own peculiar, his proper act, in this common work of them all'.

Then he goes on to discuss that anointing in terms of the working of tradition. For people of his time like ours, this was a matter hotly debated. For some, the Bible contained everything. But Andrewes takes a different line:

> This way, come we to our anointing, now, by books: this book chiefly; but, in a good part also, by the books of the ancient Fathers, and lights of the Church, in whom the scent of this ointment was fresh, and the temper true; on whose writings it lieth thick, and we thence strike it off, and gather it safely.

One can see what Andrewes is trying to say: Scripture and tradition and experience intermeshing, in that order. And tradition in a particular way among the early Fathers, so beloved of him.

Next, he spends some time discussing the different ways in which the captives are released, which takes him to the weakness of human nature. Like any skilful pastor, he starts with God's love, not with our sin. The Spirit of God heals broken hearts and can do no other. But in order for this to happen, one needs to recognise how the hearts have been broken – for example, by different kinds of captivity, through bitterness, pride, fear: 'The heart (sure) is the part of all other, we would most gladly have well.'

Healing is about forgiveness. The two are closely connected. He describes three aspects of this process, which are pardon (the declaration that all is forgiven), reconciliation (the estranged brought together) and what he calls 'repropitiation' (the whole community accepting the new situation). And these operate at the personal and the collective levels, for there is no good in running away from oneself. Like Gertrude, and doubtless many others, he echoes Augustine's image of returning to the heart: 'If we would but sometimes return to the heart, return home thither and descend into ourselves. . .'

Both these themes, the threefold pattern of pardon, reconciliation and 'repropitiation', and returning to the heart, have their parallels in the *Private Prayers*:

> mercy in wrath
>> repenting him of the evil,
>> double,
>> unto pardon,
>>> reconciliation,
>>> repropitiation.

And:

> I have sinned,
>> but I am ashamed,
>> and I turn from my wicked ways,
>> and I return unto my heart,
>> and with all my heart I return unto Thee,
>> and seek thy face. . .[12]

Finally, Andrewes links the text to the sacraments, in particular
to the Eucharist, at the end. In this case, it is the 'jubilee', the
year of the Lord's favour. The two preceding sermons carefully
approach the God of eternity meeting human beings in time
and space through word and sacrament. Here, Andrewes demonstrates an exuberance that is infectious as we are drawn into the
holy of holies and plead the sacrifice of Christ in our journey
towards heaven:

> The memorial, or mystery of which sacrifice of Christ's, is ever the
> top of our mirth, and the initiation of the joy of our jubilee. Like
> as our taking the cup of salvation is the memorial of our being
> accepted, or received and taken again to salvation.

Almost aggressively he mixes language that is direct ('the top of
our mirth') with language that is biblical ('taking the cup
of salvation').

ANDREWES' LEGACY

Andrewes walks the borderlands of worship and tradition in a
manner that makes him speak to our time with an astonishingly
new voice. In particular, there are a number of aspects to his
preaching and praying that need to be taken note of now.

There is, first of all, a sense that there will always be more to
say. He can throw a text in any direction and one knows that it
will bounce back covered in gems. He does this again and again
with an almost reckless abandon. This is not to suggest that
anything goes – far from it. But one is aware of Andrewes
walking all the time in the midst of things greater than himself.
It is a quality that Francis Paget described many years ago as
'this strong patience with unfinishedness'.[13]

Then there is the strong Trinitarian consciousness which is
more than a mannerism, because it is so much part of the man
himself. The Trinity is part of the song of the angels. The
Trinity is lost – sought – and then found – on Easter morning.
The Trinity is part of the anointing of Christ to fulfil his mission
of healing and proclamation. In traditional terms, Andrewes
combines the two traditional approaches of East and West in
working out an understanding of the Trinity that 'happens' now
(as in the very Eastern-sounding approach to the anointing of
Christ) and is also expressed in the intermeshing of virtues (as

in the somewhat Augustinian approach to the glory, peace and goodwill at Christ's birth). But it never reads dryly – it evokes a response, a sense of engagement.[14]

There is, too an ecumenical vision in the man that straddles other divides – between East and West, and across the Catholic – Protestant controversies. Donald Allchin has drawn attention to this feature.[15] Andrewes seems to produce a kind of ecumenism of the mind, long before anyone dreamt of the term, and at a time when English Christianity was deeply divided. So he insists on the Bible *and* the Fathers when he preaches in Holyrood, and he keeps referring to Augustine – and he quotes, too, Basil the Great at Whitsun in 1617, as he does Peter Chrysologus on Christmas Day 1620. But tradition is not bought cheaply. It has to be worked at.

Next, Andrewes sees word and sacrament in close relationship, not as separate events that belong to different modes of activity. The word of God is sacred, whether it is read or preached upon, or known in the breaking of the bread. Similarly, if there is an argument about which is more important, Andrewes will insist, as he did on Easter Day 1620, that it is better to have both than one or other and that we should let them work as they will and not try to drive them apart. So often his sermons conclude with a reference to the Eucharist, before ending in heaven. Word and sacrament are Kingdom events.

Finally, Andrewes uses vivid imagery. Whether he is describing the angels praising the divine virtues, or Mary Magdalen stubbornly standing there and not giving up, or Jesus engaging with the pain and distress of a world desperately in need of healing, language will always be found to speak deeply and lovingly. We do the task of preaching – and Andrewes himself – a disservice if we only identify with 'the cup of salvation' without also taking in our hands 'the top of our mirth'.

Winchester Cathedral's memorial to this preacher extraordinary seems both timely and fitting.

CHAPTER SIX

Nikolai Grundtvig: Hymn-Writer Extraordinary

THE REOPENING OF A CHURCH

> Built on the rock the church does stand
> Even when steeples are falling;
> Crumbled have spires in ev'ry land,
> Bells still are chiming and calling;
> Calling the young and old to rest,
> But above all the soul distrest,
> Longing for rest everlasting.
>
> Surely in temples made with hands,
> God, the most high, is not dwelling,
> High above earth his temple stands
> All earthly temples excelling;
> Yet, he whom heav'ns cannot contain
> Chose to abide on earth with men,
> Built in our bodies his temple.
>
> We are God's house of living stones
> Builded for his habitation;
> He through baptismal grace us owns,
> Heirs of his wondrous salvation;
> Were we but two his name to tell,
> Yet, he would deign with us to dwell,
> With all his grace and his favour.
>
> Still we our earthly temples rear,
> That we may herald his praises;
> They are the homes where he draws near
> And little children embraces;
> Beautiful things in them are said,
> God there with us his cov'nant made,
> Making us heirs of his kingdom.

Here stands the font before our eyes,
Telling how God did receive us;
Th'altar recalls Christ's sacrifice
And what his table does give us;
Here sounds his word that does proclaim
Christ yesterday, today the same,
Yes, and for aye our Redeemer.

Grant then, O God, wher'er men roam,
That when the church bells are ringing,
Many in Jesus' faith may come
Where he his message is bringing;
I know mine own, mine own know me
You not the world, my face shall see:
My peace I leave with you, Amen![1]

The first time I sang this hymn was on 29 August 1965. My
parents and my sister and I were staying in my grandparents'
summer-house in Svejbaek, a village in the lake-district of central
Jutland, Denmark. The area became well known to us over the
years and we used to go to church on Sundays to the nearby
parish of Linå, a few kilometers away on the Århus-Silkeborg
road. Linå Church has always epitomised for me the Danish
country church. It was built of rugged stones in the Romanesque
era and the exterior gives an elegant picture of whitewashed
nave, apse and tower, and red-tiled roof and saddle-back tower.
At the Reformation, the nave was lengthened, and a new reredos
and pulpit were installed, but the old font was kept. All this is
in many ways a standard Danish tale.

The occasion on that Sunday morning was a festival service
to celebrate the reopening of the church after restoration work.
It was a family trip down memory lane. The retired pastor,
Alfred Blenker, walked in the procession of clergy, all looking
distinctive in their Danish ruffs. Blenker had preached to us on
numerous occasions and was a well-known figure. During the
war, he had collaborated with my grandfather, Skat Hoffmeyer,
then Bishop of Århus, in the publication of the New Testament
translated by modern Danish authors, among whom numbered
the pastor and playwright, Kai Munk, who translated Luke's
gospel and the Acts of the Apostles; and there were illustrations
by Danish artists. The next generation were in evidence, too,

and the service was taken by the new bishop, Henning Højrup, himself a Grundtvig scholar of some note.[2]

The liturgy began in the usual way, with bell-ringing, the organ voluntary, and the opening prayer led by the *kordegn* (= 'choir-deacon', a layperson), and then we launched into this powerful hymn. I did not know enough Danish then to follow its rich meaning, but I could spot the opening line's supreme appropriateness, which comes across more directly in the Danish: 'The Church, it is an old house.' Here we were, in an old building, packed with people from all over the village and beyond, making our own imprint on the church itself by being there, and by giving thanks for old things restored, as well as new things in place (the oak pews replacing some seating of the same wood but which creaked and groaned). Here we were, too, celebrating the fact of God, dwelling on high yet in our midst. And, dear to Grundtvig's own heart, in the context of the Church's liturgy – hence those references to church-bells, the preaching of the word, and the sacraments of baptism and the Eucharist. Undergirding the whole scene, too, is the strong sense of the Church as the communion of saints, the house of living stones, proclaiming a Christ who has been with his people in ages past – yesterday – and is here now – today – and will be with us for ever. The final line of the last verse in the original Danish consists of an allusion to the words spoken by the pastor at the altar-rail when each row of communicants has received the bread and wine. Making the sign of the cross with the chalice, the priest pronounces the words, 'peace be with you all.' Everything that morning seemed very Grundtvig, so Danish, yet so universal and catholic.

But the Danes have had a harder time exporting Grundtvig than their other two great nineteenth-century figures, Søren Kierkegaard and Hans Christian Andersen. This is all the more surprising in view of the influence his travels to England had upon him. In 1951, the Danish church historian, Poul Lindhardt, wrote a study of Grundtvig for the English market. And Donald Allchin has written much about Grundtvig in the years since. The Danes themselves have produced some fine studies themselves in English. And Donald Allchin helped to bring together a group of scholars from both sides of the North Sea to look at the different aspects of Grundtvig's massive work and influence, which resulted in the publication of *Heritage and Prophecy: Grundtvig and the English-Speaking World* in 1993.[3]

WHO WAS GRUNDTVIG?

Nikolai Frederik Severin Grundtvig was born on 8 September 1783 in Udby Vicarage in the south of Sjaelland, the island on which Copenhagen is situated. His father was a quiet country pastor, and it seems that it was from his powerful mother that Grundtvig inherited his more creative, temperamental streak. In 1803 he graduated from the Faculty of Theology in Copenhagen and instead of proceeding to ordination, he took up a career as a writer and private tutor, in the course of which time he began his research on Old Norse language and literature. He then turned his eyes to ordination, but after successfully preaching the (required) trial sermon, he had a religious crisis which ended in a mental collapse. In 1811, he became his father's curate, not an unusual thing for a Lutheran to do in those days, and worked in that capacity for a year. The Danish countryside was important for him and he never lost the earthy, peasant view of the world, which comes across particularly in the natural imagery of his hymnody. One can sense the healing calm of the countryside, with the fields and woods, the birds and the wind, breathing new life into a troubled spirit. His hymns frequently refer to distress and downheartedness, an example of which we saw earlier.

But his restlessness took him back to writing and translating, including the old Danish *Gesta Danorum* of the medieval writer, Saxo. In 1821, after his first marriage, he was appointed to the parish of Praestø, not far from Udby, where he had been born. After a year, he returned to Copenhagen, to join the staff of the Church of Our Saviour, a prominent building with a stairway up its steeple. (We saw reference to the 'steeple' in the same hymn.) Grundtvig had another religious crisis in 1825 when he insisted on the need for the Apostles' Creed at baptism and rejected the liberal direction that the Danish Church was taking. Foolishly, he took out a law-suit against the Bishop of Sjaelland, the Danish Church's senior prelate, who attacked Grundtvig's published position. The result was that he was placed under censorship until 1837.

But there were those who saw in Grundtvig a creative talent

that needed to be fostered. He had graduated with the highest distinction in 1803 and he was becoming well known as a writer. The King therefore gave him a scholarship to go to England in order to study Anglo-Saxon manuscripts. It was not a case of getting rid of a difficult man. It was rather about Denmark recovering her own corporate memory and self-esteem after the disaster of the Napoleonic War, which had seen her capital bombarded by Nelson, the old medieval Church of Our Lady destroyed, and had left her bankrupt. Being a prolific writer, Grundtvig's letters from England reveal a large network of contacts with scholars and academics. To take one example, on 11 June 1829, in a letter to his wife, he tells of his desire to meet the Scottish preacher, Edward Irving, as well as his need to get credit from Barings Bank.

Grundtvig's English trips were clearly of great importance to him and it has even been suggested that it was here that he discovered the importance of the present. Through a combination of studying the Anglo-Saxon epic poem *Beowulf* as well as living in a society that was changing all the time through the effects of Industrial Revolution, Grundtvig had to face up to how the past could speak to the present and look forward to the future. The relationship between history and eternity, once again, provides a vital key to the workings of a great Christian thinker. The results were in some ways remarkable. Grundtvig's identification with the 'folk' tradition led him to take part in the national assemblies, champion the use of the Faeroese language over against Danish in those islands, and pioneer the introduction of popular adult education through the 'Folk High Schools'. These are now part of Danish life and were introduced in other parts of Scandinavia, and in the Third World.

In 1893, Grundtvig was at last given the kind of job which suited him best of all. He was appointed to be pastor of Vartov Hospital Church in Copenhagen. It was not a parish, so that he was not burdened with responsibilities which would have taken him away from his literary and national interests. But it gave him a base from which to preach and celebrate the sacraments. One of my forebears, Frederik Christian Bertelsen, who was later ordained, worked as a bookseller in Copenhagen in the late 1850s. He knew both Hans Christian Andersen, who used to visit his shop regularly, and Grundtvig himself, whom he used to hear preach at Vartov Church.

Grundtvig was a member of Parliament for a number of years after the Absolute Monarchy was abolished and a democracy introduced. He was widowed twice and each time married again, shocking the English writer, John Mason Neale, because he could be so passionately in love at the age of 75! All through this hive of activity in politics, education and literature, he preached and wrote hymns, pouring them out as if there were always more to say. From 1837, he produced volumes of his hymns, intended to improve what he considered to be the somewhat thin and pedestrian repertoire of the Danish Church at the time. In these collections, there are no fewer than 1,583 hymns, which include original compositions as well as translations of Latin and Greek hymns. Slowly, many of them gained acceptance. In the present Danish hymn-book, out of a total of 754 hymns, 160 are original Grundtvig compositions, and 101 are translations. That is a higher quota than any other author. Not all of the hymns appear exactly as he wrote them nor indeed in the number of verses of the original composition. Sometimes, as we shall see, he worked on different versions of the same hymn across the years. And there is the added difficulty of translating his poetry into decent English.

One of his most direct appeals to people was his very Danishness. The nineteenth century was not a happy time for his country. We have already alluded to the effects of the Napoleonic Wars. The other main question was Denmark's relationship with Germany. Denmark did her best to retain to the monarchy the twin-duchies of Schleswig and Holstein, but in 1864 the Prussian troops invaded them and Denmark did not stand a chance, losing a well-populated Danish-speaking part of the duchy to Germany. When the Danish-speaking congregations in Schleswig produced their own hymn-book in 1889, Grundtvig's hymnody was already prominent.[4]

By the time he died, on 2 September 1872, Grundtvig was a truly venerated figure, having left his imprint on many aspects of national life. The Church which had censored him as a young upstart in 1826 gave him the unusual recognition by conferring on him the title of honorary bishop in 1861. There is no doubt that he made an immense contribution to Denmark's quest for spiritual identity (in the broadest sense), through a time of great change. By awakening in people a kind of 'folk-memory' of the past, he gave them strength to foresee a new future by facing the present in all its human complexity.

GRUNDTVIG'S HYMNS

The first thing to say about Grundtvig's hymns is that they arise from a religious culture in which the hymn has a central place. When one enters a Danish church for a service, the book used has the hymns at the beginning and the liturgical texts with the Bible-readings for the Sundays of the year afterwards. Moreover, the hymns are built up to beforehand and phased out afterwards by a clever and cultivated use of the organ. Choosing hymns in traditional Lutheran worship is therefore far from sprinkling a few musical items across a service in which the supposedly 'real' substance lies elsewhere. Moreover, just as we saw a careful integration of preaching and piety in Lancelot Andrewes' *Private Prayers*, so in Grundtvig there is a close correspondence between his sermons and his hymns, a fact which Christian Thodberg, a noted Grundtvig scholar, has brought out.[5] To take one example, one of my first memories of discussing Grundtvig was when my parents spoke of his love of the phrase 'bath and board' to refer to the sacraments of baptism and Eucharist. This recurs in his hymnody. But he also uses it in the prayer he wrote as a prelude to his Trinity Sunday sermon in 1838.

'Herre, hvor skal vi gå hen?'

The first hymn we shall now look at, 'Lord, where shall we go?', appears in no fewer than five versions in his published texts, from the first, in 1837, to the last in 1864. Just to show how far Grundtvig's tampering with his own work could go, it is interesting to see how in 1837 the original twelve-verse hymn is reduced to six in 1864, expanded to seven in 1862 (not the same verses as 1837), nine verses in 1862–3 (again not the same as 1837), and finally to be resolved into the six-verse version in 1864 which appears in the current Danish hymn-book. I offer here a translation in prose-poetry that tries to keep as much of the imagery and directness of the original as possible, but which reads in the style of a devotional prayer:

Lord, from you we cannot flee,
you who are the friend of souls,
the Son of the Living God.
The goal of our faith,
the only being on earth
in whose mouth is the word of life.

Your word cannot frighten us away,
even when it sounds harshly in our ears.
For we feel deep within us
that on earth death is the uniquely harsh word
and that what breathes life into it again
is bled from you as a labour of sheer love.

'Eat my flesh and drink my blood' –
says the good Prince of Life –
' – on my word, with bread and wine.
My death, it was for you.
My resurrection from the dark earth,
it was for you.'
My going ahead of you into heaven,
it was for you.

Listen, my heart, beating within my breast
with anxious thoughts.
Take Our Lord at his word, taste him
at his table of grace.
Eat his flesh and drink his blood,
and rise up, as he did, to new life.

The King of heaven's Son speaks
and bears witness:
'Anyone who shares in my flesh and blood,
with a good will has my life in him,
just as my Father's life is in me.'

This is the secret known on earth
to Jesus and his community.
The world considers it vanity,
but the heart feels
that truly down to the very dust itself
has stooped the life that dwells
in the love of God.[6]

It will be apparent from an initial glance that this hymn is soaked
in the 'Bread of Life' discourse in John's gospel (John 6). The

key verses from the gospel are as follows: 'Simon Peter answered him, "Lord, to whom shall we go? You have the words of eternal life; and we have believed, and have come to know that you are the Holy One of God" ' (John 6:68–69). The whole hymn reflects upon this chapter and does so in a meditative style. Verse 1 is a confession of faith, based on those key verses quoted above. Verse 2 mentions the 'harsh word' (John 6:60), of death, which the Spirit overcomes (cf. John 6:63). Verse 3 is the imperative formula of the Eucharist ('do this. . .'), from Jesus, the Bread of Life (John 6:35), who goes ahead into heaven (John 6:63). Verse 4 revels in *angst*, with the themes of unbelief (John 6:60ff) and being raised to new life (John 6:39). Verse 5 confronts us with the promise of Christ (John 6:53ff) and the union of the Father in the Son, of believer in the Lord, which is strong in Lutheran piety. Verse 6 rounds off the hymn with a focus on Christ as the one who empties himself and whose life is in a real sense 'hidden' from view.

So much for the direction of the hymn. What of the special Grundtvig touches? The key word is a favourite Grundtvig expression, *nådebord*, 'table of grace'. And it is this motif that suggests another way of interpreting the hymn along participatory lines. The hymn is, in fact, a eucharistic devotion, which need not surprise us, because the 'Bread of Life' discourse is a text that has been debated for centuries in regard to the Eucharist. But it avoids the passive, Good Friday approach of the Lutheran 'Pietism' of a generation earlier than Grundtvig's, and the dullness of the Enlightenment approach which Grundtvig was himself rebelling against.

On this view, the hymn can be viewed as follows: verse 1 is the approach to the altar; verse 2 is the ambivalence with which that approach can be made; verse 3 is the narrative of the Last Supper, an integral and isolated part of the Lutheran liturgy; verse 4 is the reception of communion, kneeling at the altar; verse 5 is the response to the indwelling of Christ in the Eucharist; verse 6 is that response in fellowship with other Christians.

There is a vivid quality in this hymn which is typical of the author. And yet that vividness does not spill over into the rhetoric of activism known to many Christians today. To use an image from another gospel, this hymn combines in a sublime manner the practical qualities of Martha with the reflective quali-

ties of Mary (Luke 10:38–42). Further, Grundtvig not only
recognises differences of experience, including darkness itself
(the cross raised from the 'dark earth'), but also faces head-on
the fact that some people are going to reject Christianity and
find it too much to take.

'Tie, alt kød, for åsyn hans'
We have just seen Grundtvig meditating on a well-known Bible-
text. Now we turn to a quite different side of him, the so-called
'Greek Awakening' which is manifest in the 1837 collection of
hymns. In the next chapter, we shall see just how new a path it
was for John Mason Neale to look to the East and translate
some of the ancient hymns of the Greek Church, setting in
motion a tradition that went on after him. But here is Grundtvig,
working independently of Neale – and before him – on terrain
that must have seemed quite foreign to his Danish congregations. It is not possible to emphasise too strongly the significance of this work. Indeed, the Danish scholar, Jørgen Elbeck,
has identified the very volume which Grundtvig borrowed from
the Royal Library in Copenhagen in January 1837, an eighteenth-century edition of the Greek *Leitourgikon*. But before we
look at what Grundtvig actually produced, it is necessary first to
see the original Greek hymn in its context.

> Let all mortal flesh be silent, and stand in fear and trembling, and
> harbour no earthly thoughts, for the King of Kings and Lord of
> Lords comes forth to be slain and given as food to the faithful. The
> choirs of archangels go before him, with all the principalities and
> powers, the many-eyed Cherubim and the six-winged Seraphim,
> faces covered, and proclaiming the hymn: Alleluia, Alleluia,
> Alleluia![7]

These words are well known to English-speaking Christians
through the translation by Gerald Moultrie in 1864, 'Let all
mortal flesh keep silence.' But in the Greek rite, it first appears
in the eleventh and twelfth centuries, on Holy Saturday in the
Liturgy of St Basil of Caesarea, and in the regular Sunday-by-
Sunday Liturgy of St James. Its position in these rites is important: it is the hymn sung while the gifts of bread and wine are
brought in procession from the prothesis, out through the north
door of the iconostasis, down among the people, and through

the central door to the altar. The hymn sung at this point has long been regarded as an anticipation of the Eucharist itself, in which heaven and earth bow down before the mystic presence of Christ, who comes to be slain as the victim on our behalf. In this connection, it is interesting to note that even Moultrie refrains from using the word 'slain' in his translation.[8]

What does Grundtvig make of his Greek original? The answer, very much more than a mere translation. What follows is another prose-poem translation, this time written in order to reproduce the original directly:

Keep silence, all flesh, before his face,
which becomes pale on his cross!
The eclipsed sun keeps its lustre
For his head falls,
The earth trembles, fatally,
Earth's wish from the heart here gives way
To heaven's fruit of praise!

King of Kings, Lord of lords,
Himself is the lamb of sacrifice.
The order of guests, fully eternal,
Is today appointed,
For his flesh is the food of souls,
And his blood is life from death,
The Lord's Table is heaven.

Where to the altar under a garland
That Lamb of God speaks,
Before him goes, with clouds in lustre
Heaven's crowd of angels,
Cherubim with gentle eyes,
Seraphim with white wings,
Sings subdued, deep Alleluia!

At the sight eyes are closed,
Sun and Seraphim close their eyes,
Dare not look on anger's flesh,
In the hours of darkness;
Even souls that are saved do that,
Close their eyes, believe, and kneel,
Sigh deep Alleluia!

Wisdom becomes upturned on earth,
God's little wisdom found.
Therefore now the word of God's grace
May sound like folly;
Those who will not miss heaven,
God is bound to embrace in his folly,
And sigh deep Alleluia![9]

From the outset, it is obvious that Grundtvig uses the original hymn as a way of producing a quite different effect. Instead of human beings hailing the arrival of the eucharistic Christ in awesome silence, the picture painted is a combination of different elements, all to do with the juxtaposition of the truth of heaven and the human condition. The sequence of ideas is as follows. Verse 1 has the earth in silence before the cosmic happenings that accompany Christ's death in Matthew's gospel (Matt. 27:45, 51). Verse 2 then sets the Eucharist in heaven (Rev. 17:14) as well as on earth (Luke 14:16) and rejoices in the sheer fact of Christ's flesh and blood as the food and drink at the Lord's table. Verse 3 keeps the heavenly focus (Rev. 5:6–14) through the image of the altar, and the Eucharist as the earthly celebration of the heavenly reality. Verse 4 draws together the attitude of the heavenly beings with those of humans, for the eucharistic worshipper on earth also closes eyes, believes and bows. Verse 5 takes up another Grundtvig theme, the foolishness of God and the wisdom of the world (1 Cor. 1:21), and with gentle irony trusts the promise of God's word.

There is a unity about this hymn which shows Grundtvig at his most original. The constant repetition of and contrast between heaven and earth results in both being affected: heaven absorbs earth and earth absorbs heaven. Heavenly beings become a model of reverence for those who look to Christ in faith. The eucharistic food, too, is not confined to a rite or a procedure. There is a strong sense of the mystery of the Lord's Supper. The original Greek has been twisted and turned and added to and adapted, but its essential message is maintained. There is almost a sensuous quality about the thrice-repeated 'Alleluia' at the end of each of the last three verses – Grundtvig's own way of reproducing the threefold cry in the original.

'Kaerligheds og Sandheds Ånd'

The next hymn also comes from the 1837 collection, and this time the source of inspiration is one of the hymns of Adam of St Victor, who was a canon of the Abbey of St Victor in Paris, and who died probably about the year 1177. Like Grundtvig, he liked to write on the grand scale. What Grundtvig composed by way of free improvisation on Adam's sequence, *'Qui procedis ab utroque'* (= 'who proceeds from each', i.e. the Holy Spirit) is perhaps one of the richest hymns written on the Holy Spirit.

> Spirit of love and truth
> You alone knit together
> The heart-ligaments of earth and heaven;
> Endow us with a beautiful voice.
> Deep within our hearts
> Make your pure flame glow.
>
> Let what is revealed to you be known,
> Your bright light is gentle and clear;
> It is the splendour of the heart.
> You are the meaning of love.
> Your virtue is true purity,
> blessedness is your crown.
>
> Only the gentle do you make clever,
> Only the good do you call to your feast,
> Only the meek do you strengthen,
> For the royal road is peace;
> Your whole way of life is righteousness
> Cunning and violence are plagues to you.
>
> Where you shine, darkness vanishes,
> All indecency is shunned,
> Mocked by your grace;
> Truth, like the light of day,
> Crowns the riddle of love
> In the gathering of your friends.
>
> In the great bath of the soul
> And in the drink and food of the heart,
> You are the power of God's nature;
> In every branch and in every spray
> On the true vine, Christ,
> You are the sap of life.

With a good conscience
To the little ones you descend
And produce pure joys.
Make them shine and clean,
until they stand before the God of light
In snow-white clothes.

Baal never lights your fire.
Nor does it blaze with a wild flame.
Up to a head of heat
You glow, you flame, you only melt,
gentle in the heart, sweet in the mouth
as God's love.

You, as from the little flock,
Weak and shy and fearful,
Won great struggles.
Make now of us an army,
which will dare to swing the sword of
the Spirit under the sign of the cross.

Love for this earth, you see,
Is to be wounded a great deal,
Its blaze burns fiercely.
Put it out with gentle dew,
Let us blaze from the fire
You light for heaven!

On our every night and night
We stare with delight
Which disturbs the peace;
Let us one and all fall in love
With Jesus as our life and light
Which makes for unity.[10]

   The first point to notice about this hymn is that it uses
Scripture far less than the previous one. There is a reference to
Christ as the vine (John 15:15) in verse 5, to Christ's 'little flock'
(Luke 12:32) in verse 8, and to unity in the Lord (John 17:21)
in the final verse. Then the hymn itself bears little relation to
Adam of St Victor's original, except in general terms. Both
hymns reflect on the experience of the Holy Spirit in virtues, in
the clash of good and evil, and in the givenness of the Spirit
in the life of faith. In that they are at one, and both go off in

different directions to explore these themes. But there are significant differences. Whereas Adam of St Victor alludes in general terms of the sacraments in one line, Grundtvig gives more space over to baptism and Eucharist. 'The great bath of the soul' (verse 5) leads into the 'drink and food of the heart', culminating in an image which is vivid to the point of aggressive, 'you are the sap of life.' And in the following verse, baptism is seen in bold, salvific terms, expressing Christ's 'descent' for his little ones, the 'snow-white clothes' being the baptismal garments.

Present, too, are the themes of conflict. Near the start, with the virtues, then in the middle, with the stark mention of Baal, in contrast to the heavenly Spirit, and finally in the *necessity* of suffering in verse 9: 'Love for this earth . . . is to be wounded a great deal.' So strongly does Grundtvig feel this truth that he almost exaggerates the point he is making in the final verse when he suggests that gazing at heaven means having peace which disturbs our lives! Yet the passion is there, for to stare at heaven results in falling in love with Christ. A suggestion of the conflict that is part of the life of faith lies in a very Grundtvig word, 'the *riddle* of love' (verse 4). Revelation is not obvious but has the character of mystery about it.

One of the main differences between Grundtvig and Adam of St Victor is that whereas Adam takes care to speak of the Spirit proceeding from the Father and the Son, a key-note of the concluding doxological verse in the Latin original, Grundtvig speaks direct to the Spirit and weaves his work into creation and redemption with an almost relentless energy. The Spirit creates – and redeems. The Spirit is known in love and truth but also in the conflicts that are inherent in fallen, human life; and he is also at work in the sacraments, where the created order is used and blessed in order to become vehicles of the kingdom of heaven. (I have sung this very hymn on different occasions in Århus Cathedral at the font and also during the distribution of communion at the altar.) To see in the Holy Spirit the 'heart-ligaments' that bind earth and heaven together is to have an understanding of the work of God that is Spirit-filled – and creation-focused.

GRUNDTVIG – HERITAGE AND PROPHECY?

Grundtvig is rich fare. He is idiosyncratic. And it is plain from the energy with which he wrote and the determination with which he spoke of the darker side of human experience that he was one of those highly creative figures who had a deeply sensitive nature. He stands in some contrast with Andrewes, the self-contained contemplative, whose fire would break out in the pulpit, but whose reserve would probably be more apparent at the personal level. The all-embracing character of Grundtvig's writings has more in common with Augustine, with his passionate nature and his slightly unpredictable use of language which could be at once simple to the point of being plain, and also complex to the point of being tortuous. One senses, frankly, a mind that seldom stands still, but is all the time energetically reaching out for more, in order to express more, and doing so whether the literary product is clear or obtuse.

He is, above all, a man whose very national and cultural contexts makes him a very Danish Dane and also a figure steeped in the Romantic Movement,[11] with his love of the imagination, his reverence for the past, and his creative vision for turning the present into a glorious future. Moreover, his hymn translations include those of Isaac Watts and James Montgomery, which shows that he was searching for material among his contemporaries and near-contemporaries, and not just in the Latin and Greek past. When he basks in Scripture and produces a hymn on the journey of faith to the Lord's Table; or when he steeps himself in an ancient Greek hymn and plucks from it exactly what he wants to unite heaven and earth through the cross with the sun's eclipse over the crucified Lord; and when he dips into a lengthy hymn by a medieval writer with equally prolix tendencies and through his own ingenuity and vision manages to write one of the most tantalising hymns to the Holy Spirit ever written – when he goes to these lengths (and more) we know that we are in the presence of a man who transcends many of the conventional divisions of Christianity.

The more an author writes, the more recognisable he becomes through favourite themes and images, as we have already noted. The 'bath and board' motif that he used in pulpit and in song is clearly one such. And in the current Danish hymn-book there are no fewer than seven of his hymns that use this expression.[12]

But repetition – 'iteration' – is part of the business of the Gospel, which has its effects. For Grundtvig's preaching and hymnody inculcated into the Danish Church not only a more frequent Sunday eucharistic celebration (it is the almost universal norm to celebrate the Lord's Supper every Sunday) but a higher and more reverent view of the sacrament of baptism. Other churches might well follow that example, perhaps offsetting eucharistic inflation by hallowing the font as well as the altar through sacred song.

But Grundtvig would want us to do more than simply read him. Among the old family photographs in my possession is a battered black-and-white of the great man himself, sitting in old age in pensive mood. He had lived to see a great deal and had experienced controversy – not always well handled by himself! – as he sought to steer the church he loved so much away from what he saw as the perils of extreme liberalism, in which the Christian faith is relativised out of existence, and pietism, in which a false evangelical fervour can subject that faith to individualism and emotionalism. But what he gives in return is no easy option, for he himself, as Donald Allchin has recently written, 'continues to amaze and perplex us'. And he goes on, 'the elements of continuity in his life are at least as strong as the elements of change.[13]

His vision is wide and deep. He walks confidently and creatively through all manner of sources and traditions. And he takes from his heritage – and ours – a wealth of reflection and conveys it in the form of sacred verse that can leap from the pages of the Danish hymn-book and walk with the worshipper into the future equipped with prayerful song, the word of God, and the sacraments of the Gospel.[14]

CHAPTER SEVEN

Two Nineteenth-Century Contrasts:
John Mason Neale and Christina Rossetti

John Mason Neale
A COMPLINE HYMN

Before the ending of the day,
Creator of the world, we pray,
That with thy wonted favour thou
Wouldst be our guard and keeper now.

From all ill dreams defend our eyes,
From nightly fears and fantasies;
Tread under foot our ghostly foe,
That no pollution we may know.

O Father, that we ask be done,
Through Jesus Christ thine only Son,
Who, with the Holy Ghost and thee,
Doth live and reign eternally.[1]

Whenever I hear this hymn, I think of the Office of Compline
and a small group of people. Perhaps we are together for a
meeting or a study group, which is concluded by someone passing round some tattered copies of one of the various versions of
that service which have been in circulation in recent times.
Images flow past; the day that has gone, the discussion that has
just taken place, and the journey home, with the prospect of the
next day and all that it might bring. The hymn is so integral to
Compline that it sometimes seems hard to think of any other
association. Indeed, this is so firmly embedded in my mind that
I can remember occasions when, as a boy, the group was so small
and the context so inappropriate for singing that we actually *said*
it instead of leaving it out!

The Office of Compline goes back centuries and has changed

little in the West until the more radical recent revisions with their alternatives. The precise origins are obscure, but it is possible to gain a vague picture of how it developed.[2] In the 'Rule' of Basil of Caesarea, we find the following direction: 'At the beginning of the night we ask that our rest may be without offence and free from fantasies, and at this hour also Psalm 91 must be recited.'

Three vital pieces of information can be gleaned from this brief sentence: there was a form of prayer for all monks last thing at night; Psalm 91 ('Whoso dwelleth under the defence of the Most High') is an integral part of it; and its purpose is to commend the night to God and to ask to be freed from fantasies. If one compares Basil's words, written in the East in the second part of the fourth century, with the hymn just quoted, which was written in the West, probably in the seventh century, there is an exact correspondence. It would seem that the hymn, beginning in Latin '*Te lucis ante terminum*', complete with its concluding doxology, carries the purpose of Compline in every syllable. Economic in expression, it begins by turning to God and asking for his favour at the end of the day. It continues to ask in specific terms for deliverance from temptation and fantasy – for celibate monks these would seem obvious, though there are similar ones for married people as well. And it ends in the traditional manner by offering praise to God the Holy Trinity.

There have been other Compline hymns in the West but this is the most stable. It did not survive the English Reformation, though the Song of Simeon, the 'Nunc Dimittis', together with some other elements such as the Apostles' Creed and the Confession, were absorbed into the new Office of Evening Prayer. But it remained part of Catholic tradition and became popular in the English-speaking world when it appeared in 1851 in this simple and effective translation by a brilliant versifier, John Mason Neale.

WHO WAS JOHN MASON NEALE?[3]

John Mason Neale was born in 1818, the son of Cornelius Neale, a London Evangelical priest who wore himself out to an early death. In 1836, the young Neale went up to Trinity College, Cambridge, and made long walks – not sport – his hobby. He had a natural talent for writing prose and composing in verse, and these gifts were apparent at an early age. In fact, he was prolific at both. At Cambridge he founded with his friend, Benjamin Webb, the Cambridge Camden Society, which was intended to stir up interest in medieval church architecture and to awaken people to the need to repair – or even rebuild – the architectural heritage of the nation, which in many places had fallen into sometimes tragic disrepair. Neale was thus associated at the start of his career with implementing on a practical level ideals which were stirring as part of a wider movement. But his contribution was far wider still.

At Oxford, the search for Anglican roots bore fruit with the Tractarians, in their desire to recover the theological past and enrich the Church of England by awakening people to her collective memory. At Cambridge, the fruits were equally tangible, and equally controversial. At the time, the two centres with their historic and happy rivalries could afford a certain self-consciousness at how different these two aspects were. With the benefit of hindsight, we can see that they merge into each other. Both were essentially about *creative recovery* of the past. Neale and Webb remained firm friends for the rest of Neale's life and they wrote to each other frequently, sometimes several times a week. Such relationships of theological friendship have always been important.

When it came to finding a job in the Church, Neale was less than lucky. He served for a very short time as Curate of St Nicolas, Guildford, but Bishop Charles Sumner of Winchester refused to license him because his views on how churches should look and what services should be like were well known through his publications. After marriage in 1842 to Sarah Webster, the daughter of a Cambridge vicar, he went to Crawley, Sussex, to try his hand at being a country priest. Here he suffered a breakdown in health and on doctor's orders he moved to Madeira, where he wintered regularly in the early 1840s. Funchal, on the south-east coast of Maderia, with its fine fifteenth-century cathedral, was to make a powerful impression on him. He learnt Portuguese and had the run of the seminary library. He became acquainted with native Catholicism and made friends wherever he went. He used for his own devotions Lancelot Andrewes' *Private Prayers*, a further indication of his commitment to unlock the gates of tradition to a church badly in need of it. More spectacularly, he translated Andrewes' prayers into Portuguese in 47 days between October and December 1843! It is sometimes blandly asserted that travel broadens the mind. There can be little doubt that Neale's life in Madeira and his journey much later to Dalmatia in 1861 affected him profoundly. He had a love of the past, but he had an innovative approach to the present. For him, living at a time when the future of the Church of England was much debated, it was important to know in a personal as well as an academic manner the traditions of Western and Eastern Christianity.

Like Grundtvig, whom he in some ways resembles, he was too unusual a person to fit into normal categories. A proper job had to be found for him where he could be part of a community, carry on his studies, and be enabled to give the wider Church the kind of influence that it needed. In 1847, he was offered the Wardenship of Sackville College, East Grinstead. This was an almshouse with a seventeenth-century foundation. No warden before him had been ordained. But there was a chapel with regular services and a secure future. It was an ingenious move and, although he was for some time prevented from officiating by the Bishop of Chichester because of his advanced liturgical practices, it worked out well. He could write to his heart's content, and that included novels about life in the East, not a subject one would expect from a clergyman of his stature. Those who heard him preach noted three characteristics about him: the power of his personality, his sense of contemporaneity with the saints, and his colourful use of background information.

All these three features shine through in his wider ministry. He had a relentless ability to get material on paper and from his pen there poured forth a whole series of publications. In 1851, he published his *Mediaeval Hymns and Sequences* which contains a series of hymns that are now part and parcel of the normal repertoire of English-speaking churches all round the world: to take but two examples, 'The royal banners onward go', written by Venantius Fortunatus in the sixth century, 'All glory, laud and honour' perhaps by Theodulf of Orleans in the ninth. Much more innovative, however, was his *Hymns of the Eastern Church*, which appeared in 1862. We shall be looking at specimens of both these works later.

A comparison has already been drawn with Grundtvig, whom

Neale met on one occasion. Both had a passionate interest in
the wider Christian inheritance and both wanted to communi-
cate this inheritance, by adaptation, to the Church of their day.
And both achieved this by writing, and preaching, and through
the medium of the hymn. In Grundtvig's case, the hymn was an
already-existing and much-valued feature of the worship of his
church. Not so with Neale. Hymns had been sung off and on
since the Reformation in Anglican worship, and the Psalter was
known by many – perhaps most – through its metrical versions.
In the previous century, Methodism had been born in song,
exalting the hymn through the compositions of the Wesley
brothers to a position in English worship perhaps unknown
before.

Neale understood the potential of the hymn and this, coupled
with his ready ability at versification, probably explains why he
was both so determined in this regard and so successful. He
seems to have inherited much of this enthusiasm from his Evangelical roots. But he met prejudice, not least from Webb who
on one occasion wrote to him suggesting firmly that any hymns
sung in Anglican worship should be in Latin, an idea ridiculous
today but entertained seriously by some educated people then.
Neale wrote back, 'Why not have English hymns, if we have
English prayer?' And so Neale wrote hymns, for the young (he
always loved children), for the sick (he instinctively sympathised
with those chronically ill because of his own ill health), as well
as other original compositions that included carols. But his main
legacy – and it is considerable – lies in his translations from the
Latin and the Greek.

His interest in the Eastern churches was another bone of
contention. When he embarked on what he himself regarded as
his main life's work, *The History of the Holy Eastern Church*, Webb
expressed the view commonly held at the time that the East was
not quite acceptable and proper: 'I do fear your Orientalizing. I
trust you will write Greek history on high Occidental ground.'
As Leon Litvack has shown in his recent study of Neale's works
on the Eastern Church, Neale was taking a far bolder step than
we who live in a more ecumenically conscious age understand.[4]

Two other aspects of Neale's work should be noted. One is
his interest in the presentation of the liturgy, where he was
avowedly Western. He pioneered the use of the chasuble at a

daily Eucharist at a time when it was even disowned by some of the Oxford Fathers. Moreover, his concern about architecture and church interiors gave him a name for proposing reorderings (as they would be called today) that reflected a more medieval pattern. Thus at Sackville College, and with the nursing sisterhood at East Grinstead (another pioneering project) the altar was the central focus rather than the pulpit and elaborate decoration filled the sanctuary. In this activity, Neale made no attempt whatever to adopt Eastern practices of any kind, even though he knew them, had seen them and understood something of their origins and development.[5] He understood that while religious cultures can vary and grow and absorb new ideas and practices, they still needed to build on an existing framework. For him, the Anglican pattern had its roots going back to before the Reformation, and in this evolution the East was an important and neglected cousin from which we have a great deal to learn but not on which we could remodel ourselves.

The other area of Neale's interest concerns specifically liturgical work. In 1859, Neale published a collection of translations of five of the ancient Eastern liturgies, a remarkable little book which brought to a wider public texts known to scholars through Latin versions and Greek originals.[6] This was one of the first liturgical books I ever read. And in two appendices, Neale tackles two controversial areas by providing sample texts from yet more liturgies. First, the different kinds of narrative of the institution of the Eucharist (67 texts are given) and then prayers for the departed. It is clear from his whole approach that he is more interested in style and form than in shape and idea. His collected articles on the history of liturgy show the same priorities.[7]

At the end of a life packed full of activity, with its punishing daily schedule, Neale died in 1866. But he left a great deal behind him, and it is to his hymns that we must now turn.

NEALE'S HYMNS

'Urbs beata Jerusalem'

This hymn may well date back to the ninth century and was probably composed for the dedication of churches, an industry that had a ready market as the Middle Ages progressed. It came to be associated with the dedication festival of a church. In

England during the reign of Henry VIII before the separation
from Rome, it was decreed that every church that did not have
a known dedication date should hold this festival on the first
Sunday in October.

Neale's translation appeared in 1851 in the *Mediaeval Hymns
and Sequences*. It comes in nine verses like the Latin original.
The versions sung today are the result of editing and abbrevi-
ation. For example, often only the last five verses are sung.
Neale's instinctive grasp of metre at times feels as if he is reproducing the measure of the Latin with a simple boldness. Here
are those verses with Grundtvig's version following:

Neale (1851)

Christ is made the sure foundation,
  And the precious Corner-stone,
Who, the two-fold walls surmounting,
  Binds them closely into one:
Holy Sion's help for ever,
  And her confidence alone.

All that dedicated City,
  Dearly lov'd by God on high,
In exultant jubilation
  Pours perpetual melody;
God the One, and God the Trinal,
  Singing everlastingly.

To this Temple, where we call Thee,
  Come, O Lord of Hosts, to-day!
With Thy wonted loving-kindess
  Hear Thy people as they pray;
And Thy fullest benediction
  Shed within its walls for aye.

Here vouchsafe to all Thy servants
  That they supplicate to gain:
Here to have and hold for ever
  Those good things their prayers obtain;
And hereafter in Thy Glory
  With Thy blessed ones to reign.

Laud and honour to the Father;
  Laud and honour to the Son;
Laud and honour to the Spirit;

Ever Three, and ever One:
Consubstantial, Co-eternal,
  While unending ages run.

Grundtvig (1837)

On the new Jerusalem
Which the King from Bethlehem,
By His Word has founded,
We must build with faith and pray'r,
By His Spirit's loving care,
And God's grace unbounded.

Its foundations prais'd alone
As the church's cornerstone,
We are all extolling;
It is Jesus Christ the Lord,
Who a refuge shall afford,
Though the stars be falling.

He who nothing dead condones,
Will of us as living stones
Build His holy temple,
Which upon its base will rise
Like a tree, whose root supplies
It with nurture ample.

Grant, O Lord, Thy church may rest
On its true foundation blest
And its faith not alter.
Fill it with Thy light and pow'r
With Thy graces it embower,
Never let it falter.

With Thy friends, us ever rate,
And despite our lowly state,
Deign with us to tarry.
Let Thy peace in us abide.
And, when comes the eventide,
To Thy joy us carry.[8]

Comparisons are not always fair; the Latin has to be taken for granted, and the English translation of Grundtvig misses a great deal of the original. However, given these limitations, certain features spring out.

First of all, Neale's translation is much more faithful to the original. Each verse reproduces exactly the ideas and images of the Latin. Occasionally, he introduces his own. For example, in verse 4, 'to have and to hold', which in later editions becomes 'retain', is a clear echo of the marriage vow in the Book of Common Prayer. But the sequence of thought is not altered. Christ is the foundation, coming down from heaven, and he is called upon to come into 'this temple', the Church, the community of faithful in this particular building. The imagery of architecture, which would have been dear to Neale's heart in any case, is played out to the full. And the final verse reproduces the doxology of the original to perfection. The translation has energy and drive and solidity. It is a work of art in itself. And repetitive use is bound to have had its effect on generations of worshippers.

Grundtvig, however, is much freer with the original. This should be no surprise in view of what we have already seen of his work. The spiritual temple becomes internalised but never becomes individualistic. God builds the new Jerusalem by his word and Spirit, a refuge for those whose 'hearts are falling' – the motif of human anguish in Grundtvig which we have already seen. The living image of a tree appeals to him, as the hymn moves on with a prayer for the life of the Church to live the faith truly and finally to enjoy the bliss of heaven.

Between the lines we can discern two quite different possibilities. Grundtvig, on the one hand, pours out his thoughts with the Latin original as inspiration and his over-active imagination and favourite theological themes breaking in on the scene. Neale, however, is more disciplined, more reverent towards the original, anxious to bring the collective memory of the past into the present in a more accurate form. There is a precision about his version that has its own attractiveness. He is the servant of the Latin, Grundtvig certainly is not.

'Oh the mystery, passing wonder'
Neale published this translation in his volume of Eastern hymns. The principal difference for Neale is that whereas Latin hymns were in rhyming verse, Eastern hymns are not. The original is a troparia attributed to Andrew of Crete, who was made Archbishop of Crete in 712 and is one of the great hymn-

writers of the Eastern Church. This particular series is sung at
the end of Compline on the Wednesday of Holy Week, hence the
eucharistic overtones. In fact Neale translated only five of
the eight troparia. I set out below Neale's translation and following it a modern translation by two prominent Orthodox
Christians:

Neale's translation:

> Oh, the myst'ry, passing wonder,
>   When, reclining at the board,
> 'Eat,' Thou saidst to Thy Disciples
>   'That True Bread with quick'ning stor'd
> 'Drink in faith the healing Chalice'
>   'From a dying God outpour'd.'

> Then the glorious upper chamber
>   A celestial tent was made.
> When the bloodless rite was offer'd,
>   And the soul's true service paid,
> And the table of the feasters
>   As an altar stood display'd.

> Christ is now our mighty Pascha,
>   Eaten for our mystic bread;
> Take we of His broken Body,
>   Drink we of the Blood He shed.
> As a lamb led out to slaughter,
>   And for this world offered.

> To the Twelve spake Truth eternal,
>   To the Branches spake the Vine;
> 'Never more from this day forward
>   'Shall I taste again this wine,
> 'Till I drink it in the kingdom
>   'Of My Father, and with Mine.'

> Thou hast stretch'd those hands for silver
>   That had held th' Immortal Food.
> With those lips, that late had tasted
>   Of the Body and the Blood,
> Thou hast giv'n the kiss, O Judas;
>   Thou hast heard the woe bestow'd.

> Christ to all the world gives banquet
>   On that most celestial Meat;

Him, albe't with lips all earthly,
    Yet with holy hearts we greet;
Him the sacrificial Pascha,
    Priest and Victim all complete.

Mother Mary and Kallistos Ware's version:

Sitting at supper with Thy companions
O Lord who lovest mankind,
Thou hast revealed to them the great mystery
of Thine Incarnation, saying:
'Eat the living Bread, drink with faith the Blood
shed from My divine side at My death.'

The upper room wherein Christ kept the Passover
was revealed as a heavenly tabernacle;
the supper without shedding of blood
is our reasonable worship;
the table on which the Mysteries were celebrated,
there is our spiritual altar.

Christ is now our great and honoured Passover,
eaten as bread and slain as a Lamb.
He has been offered as a sacrifice for us,
and mystically we all receive with reverence
His Body and His Blood.

Christ the true Vine spoke to His Branches,
the apostles, saying: 'Amen.
I will not drink henceforth from the vine
until I drink it new with you,
My heirs in the glory of My Father.'

For thirty pieces of silver thou dost sell
Him who is above all price;
and dost thou not think, wicked Judas,
of the mystery of the Supper
and the holy washing of the feet?
O how hast thou fallen utterly
from the light, embracing with love
the hangman's noose.

Christ, the divine and heavenly Bread,
gives food to all the world.
Come, then, O lovers of Christ,

and in our mouths of clay but pure hearts
let us receive in faith the Passover
which is sacrificed and offered in our midst.[9]

It will be immediately apparent that Neale's verse translation
and the prose version by Mother Mary and Kallistos Ware contain very similar numbers of words. The only place where there
is a discrepancy is where Neale is unwilling or unable to force
the original into the verse-structure he has chosen, which is
in the fifth verse, where Judas' fate is alluded to as well as the
ceremony of the foot-washing which was unknown in Neale's
Anglicanism of the time but familiar to Andrew of Crete's mon-
astic environment. Then there are one or two places where
Neale over-translates. At the end of the first verse, there is an
expression which is almost impossible to render in English –
even Mother Mary and Kallistos Ware's version does not quite
manage it! The Greek means, literally, 'emptied from the slaugh-
ter of the side of God'. Clearly an allusion to the piercing of
the side of Christ (John 19:34ff), the original inspires Neale to
opt for simplicity, 'a dying God'. Then in the second verse he
refers to the 'bloodless rite', whereas the original Greek uses the
expression 'bloodless (better translated as "unbloody") meal'. It
is common coin in the Eastern liturgies to refer to the Eucharist
as an 'unbloody sacrifice'.[10] It was a way of showing that the
Eucharist is a sacrifice without the shedding of blood, particularly appropriate in the context of Holy Week, where the Passover imagery draws the mind towards the unleavened bread of
the Paschal meal.

But what of the hymn in general? Leon Litvack has shown
how Neale was less able to translate as accurately from Greek as
from Latin originals, and even on occasion has his own editorial
touches, such as playing down the role of the Virgin Mary –
clearly not a winner for typical Anglicans of his day. In this
hymn he is less uncomfortable about drawing the ideas into
verse. One wonders if his choice of this magnificent hymn were
not in part motivated by his achievement ten years earlier of
translating Aquinas' '*Pange lingua gloriosi*' ('Of the glorious Body
telling').[11] The atmosphere and the imagery are close, an indication for Neale of a unified tradition which knows diversity at
the sacrament of unity, the Eucharist. The main differences are

that Aquinas' hymn was written for the feast of Corpus Christi, like the prayers discussed in an earlier chapter. This particular hymn, however, is for Holy Week, which explains the Passover imagery and the words which Christ speaks as Vine to branches (John 15:5) that he will not drink of this cup until he does so in the Kingdom (Matt. 26:29), and the moving words that absorb the 30 pieces of silver.

WHAT OF NEALE?

John Mason Neale is part of a great movement in the nineteenth century that sought to recover the past in order to make it accessible to people of his day. Everything about him was of a piece. He was an individualist, who was found the right niche in which to dwell as a holy man, surrounded by his books, his letters, and a group of elderly people who came to love him. His sermons are direct in their language and conscious of the kind of people he was addressing, as well as manifestly aware of human needs and observant of the foibles of those nearby. Like Grundtvig, he was an enthusiast for those areas of history that would otherwise be neglected, hence his espousal of the Eastern liturgies and hymns. It is unfortunate that the latter have not proved more popular. 'The day of resurrection' and 'Come, ye faithful, raise the strain', both of them from John Damascus' Easter cycle, are the two exceptions.

But like all gifted people who produce a great deal, his legacy has been appreciated more and more as time has gone on. Many of his original compositions in hymnody have faded as his translations have increased in popularity. And his treatment of liturgical studies shows a healthy openness to elements of language and style that need to be appropriated in our own day as the liturgy-making industry enters new phases. He stands as an influential giant on the nineteenth-century scene, affecting *how* people worship through his hymnody, *where* they worship through his interest in architectural setting, and *why* they worship, through his deeper concerns that prayer and tradition are neither ends in themselves nor merely human activity. That sense of being contemporary with the saints which he conveyed to his hearers when he preached can never be phoney. He was aware of the life of heaven, and felt history bulged with little glimpses of it. And that was enough.

Christina Rossetti

REMEMBERING POETRY

> Passing away, saith the World, passing away:
> Chances, beauty and youth sapp'd day by day:
> Thy life never continueth in one stay.
> Is the eye waxen dim, is the dark hair changing to gray
> That hath won neither laurel nor bay?
> I shall clothe myself in Spring and bud in May:
> Thou, root-stricken, shalt not rebuild thy decay
> On my bosom for aye
> Then I answer'd: Yea.
>
> Passing away, saith my Soul, passing away:
> With its burden of fear and hope, of labour and play,
> Hearken what the past doth witness and say:
> Rust in thy gold, a moth is in thine array,
> A canker is in thy bud, thy leaf must decay.
> At midnight, at cockcrow, at morning, one certain day,
> Lo, the Bridegroom shall come and shall not delay:
> Watch thou and pray.
> Then I answered: Yea.
>
> Passing away, said my God, passing away:
> Winter passeth after the long delay:
> New grapes on the vine, new figs on the tender spray,
> Turtle calleth turtle in Heaven's May.
> Though I tarry, wait for me, trust me, watch and pray.
> Away, come away; night is past, and lo, it is day;
> My love, my sister, my spouse, thou shalt hear me say –
> Then I answer'd: Yea.[12]

These words were written in 1860 when Christina Rossetti turned 30. It was a momentous age in those days for an unmarried woman, for it usually meant final resignation to what was then termed spinsterhood. In Rossetti's case it was particularly poignant for two reasons. She was very beautiful, albeit in a striking rather than a conventionally pretty way. More to the point, Rossetti had a dark side to her personality that runs through much of her poetry. Had she ever got over not being able to marry James Collinson? Did she refuse him because he became a Roman Catholic? Or could she not quite face up to marriage because, as Jan Marsh has suggested in her recent literary biography, she may have been sexually abused by her somewhat eccentric father, Gabriele Rossetti, the unsuccessful academic? Did this explain the breakdown she appears to have had at the age of 14? When she died on 29 December 1894, after a life that had known much emotional and physical suffering, she left behind her a collection of poetical works of innate beauty and candour.[13]

These are questions that are properly asked, particularly around the centenary of her death, and at a time when the women's movement has enabled the rest of us to view the past from a fresh perspective. If you mentioned Christina Rossetti to me when I was a boy, I would have replied that she was one of the few poets whose work I could memorise without feeling terrified that I would make a mess of public recitation at school the next day. I have always found it hard to remember poetry by heart and the traditional way of 'learning poems' bred in me a nervousness about poetry as a natural consequence. But Rossetti was, for some inexplicable reason, different. She writes with simplicity, directness, realism. She also expressed a bitter-sweet introspection.

In many respects, 'Passing Away' epitomises Rossetti. She has turned her back on being young but she does so in faith. She mixes the images of the turtle-dove in the Song of Songs (2:11–14) with that of the Bridegroom coming (Matt. 25:1). But it is as if she were insisting that if the Christian faith is to have any reality to it, then the life of grace and the life of nature have to be joined together and not kept apart. For a beautiful lady who has not been able to marry this means accepting young beauty giving birth to an older beauty, and slow natural decay. For a person who is struggling to make sense of her faith it means constantly accepting in a struggling rather than a resigned fashion that there are some things in this life which are not going to change.

As our age looks back on hers, it is not hard to see that life would be different were Christina Rossetti alive now. She would have married. Her artistic circle, surrounded by pre-Raphaelites including her brother, Dante Rossetti, would have been even more open to women taking an active and public role, rather than sitting in the background doing good works of charity among fallen women and writing poetry against a background of having to prove oneself against the odds. But different ages provide their own solutions, and in comparing Rossetti with Gertrude the Great, one cannot help seeing in Gertrude a more contented and influential figure – way back in the thirteenth century.

There has been a tendency to criticise Rossetti's poetry as repetitive or else in need of more revision than it received. Prolific authors are sometimes accused of this by those less endowed with such gifts. But Jan Marsh's study, for all that it perhaps does less than adequate justice to Rossetti's religious work (and she was a very religious person) has provided the opportunity to take a more positive view. The repetitions are 'iterations', which take us again and again into the soul, into the innermost part of the self, in order to explore feeling, meaning, pain, sorrow, love in the darkness, tenderness in the disappointments. Above all there is love and affirmation – hence the 'yea' at the end of each verse, as Rossetti moves from 'world', through 'soul', to 'God', to find greater confidence. From her portraits, the onlooker can see pain but also a smile just about ready to break out. Here is the darker side of human experience which Grundtvig was so keen on expressing.

ROSSETTI'S WORK

Christina Rossetti's literary output was vast. She was a natural versifier and she started early in life. It is impossible even to summarise it here, just as it was impossible to do the same with our other writers, whether they were writing sermons, or prayers, or hymns, or treatises. 'My tongue is the pen of a ready writer' (Ps. 45:2) is probably an adequate motto for all the people we have been looking at so far. But Rossetti forms a suitable contast to Neale, who knew her work, and quoted it in his preaching. She is a reminder that for many people life is never fulfilled and often unsatisfying. But it can still be glorious. Here are a few testimonies to this truth.

'Trinity Sunday'

> My God, Thyself being Love Thy heart is love,
> And love Thy Will and love Thy Word to us,
> Whether Thou show us depths calamitous

Or heights and flights of rapturous peace above.
O Christ the Lamb, O Holy Ghost the Dove,
    Reveal the Almighty Father unto us;
    That we may tread Thy courts felicitous,
Loving Who loves us, for our God is Love.

Lo, if our God be Love thro' heaven's long day,
    Love is He thro' our mortal pilgrimage,
Love was he thro' all aeons that are told.
We change, but Thou remainest; for Thine age
    Is, Was, and Is to come, nor new nor old;
We change, but thou remainest; yea and yea![14]

This poem is one of a series written for different occasions in
the Church year. In writing in this vein, Rossetti takes up the
mantle of George Herbert, who in characteristic fashion writes
with similar sentiments but in a more compressed style in 'Trini-
tie Sunday':

Lord, Who hast form'd me out of mud,
    And hast redeem'd me through thy bloud,
    And sanctifi'd me to do good.

Purge all my sinnes done heretofore;
    For I confesse my heavie score,
    And I will strive to sinne no more.

Enrich my heart, mouth, hands in me,
    With faith, with hope, with charitie,
    That I may runne, rise, rest with Thee.[15]

The styles are different, but both bend the Trnity into human
experience, Herbert through the confession of sin, Rossetti by
the (more characteristic) concentration on the human condition
of sin and weakness. She also widens her embrace to include
heights and depths and the fact of God's unchanging nature set
against our capacity for constant change. 'Love' (or its cognate
'loving') occurs eight times in the space of Rossetti's 14 lines, an
indication that for her it is love that makes sense of human life.

'My harvest is done'

Much of her poetry has a morbid streak and it would not be fair
to her if this were not noted. The following has been regarded
as her own epitaph as it explores one of favourite themes,

touched on in 'Trinity Sunday', the relationship between time
and eternity:

> My harvest is done, its promise is ended,
>   Weak and watery sets the sun,
> Day and night in one mist are blended,
>   My harvest is done.
>
>   Long while running, how short when run,
> Time to eternity has descended,
>   Timeless eternity has begun.
>
> Was it the narrow way that I wended?
>   Snares and pits was it mine to shun?
> The scythe has fallen, so long suspended,
>   My harvest is done.[16]

Here we have self-doubt and faith mingling together and refusing to become anomalies that are somehow ironed out by a
technology that invades from outside. It is as if she were determined not to let go of the vital human questions that have been
part of her life and which refuse to be surrendered in the
interests of blandness. 'My harvest is done' is a way of saying
that my life is over, I still have questions, but I am prepared to
let go and hand myself over from time to time into eternity.
There is no simple trust here.

A prayer

> O God of patience and consolation, grant we beseech thee that with
> free hearts we may love and serve thee and our brethren; and, having
> thus the mind of Christ, may begin heaven on earth, and exercise
> ourselves therein till that day when heaven, where love abideth,
> shall seem no strange habitation to us; for Jesus Christ's sake.[17]

Rossetti wrote many prayers and this example is a summary of
her faith. We can see ideas and emphases that appeared in
'Passing Away', 'Trinity Sunday', and 'My harvest is done'. Love,
human endurance, time and eternity – these are all brought
together with a clarity and a force that make it sound as if heaven
were here already, certainly not a country far above the blue sky
where we might just conceivably meet one day. For Rossetti,
with all her talent at writing the beautiful but sharp and memorable line, to 'begin heaven on earth' is not about turning faith

into a means of getting rid of pain. It is rather a way of facing up to that pain, working through it, and finding heaven somehow in embryo.

WHAT OF ROSSETTI?

Christina Rossetti stands outside the world of John Mason Neale, with his constant correspondents, the requests for ecclesiastical advice, and the next theological treatise which will find a ready publisher. Here is a deeply sensitive woman who like our other writers is both very much part of her own time and a figure of wider significance. She tackles the great human questions through her own experience – and her almost unending capacity to observe and not give up. Like Gertrude, she made no conscious and overt contribution to the development of Christian worship. Instead she sits by her desk and writes away. A High Anglican by upbringing, by birth a three-quarters Italian, she breathes a passionate, independent spirit that sits easily on border terrain. Through her poems and her prayers, she reaches the experience of many people. She stops religious reflection from becoming too churchy. As a woman she witnesses to the pain of women's memory and to the courage of those who used their position, their art, their flair, their creativity, to look again and again at life – and say 'yea'.

CHAPTER EIGHT

Drawing On

===

COHERENCE EMERGES

> The eagle soars in the summit of Heaven,
> The Hunter with his dogs pursues his circuit.
> O perpetual revolution of configured stars,
> O perpetual recurrence of determined seasons,
> O world of spring and autumn, birth and dying!
> The endless cycle of idea and action,
> Endless invention, endless experiment,
> Brings knowledge of motion, but not of stillness;
> Knowledge of words, and ignorance of the Word.
> All our knowledge brings us nearer to our ignorance,
> All our ignorance brings us nearer to death,
> But nearness to death no nearer to God.
> Where is the Life we have lost in living?
> Where is the knowledge we have lost in information?
> The cycles of Heaven in twenty centuries
> Bring us farther from God and nearer to the Dust.[1]

These words might well be the end of the story. They certainly ring true of many of the wearied strains of those who would throw up their arms at the whole Christian enterprise and give up, or else throw up their arms at one version of it in order to pursue it in another. 'Where is the knowledge we have lost in information?', might T. S. Eliot well ask as he begins his densely packed Choruses from 'The Rock', crying out to modern civilisation to have the heart and the patience to stand still and reflect on its true story, its search for meaning, its inner coherence. But how does 'it all' fit together? The answer depends not on the kind of church one belongs to, or the style of its worship, or even the way it is governed, though such questions as these are important and continue to delineate between various approaches to Christianity.

Thus far, we have looked at eight quite different writers. All they seem to share is the Western European legacy at different stages of its outworking. In a moment we shall look at some common threads. But for now, the starting-point has to be God – God the giver of all good gifts, God the source and final purpose of the world, God who is both autonomous from his creation and intimately involved in it, God supremely revealed in Jesus Christ, God alive in the world today through the Spirit of Life, God who coaxes human beings to look not back in anger but forward with faith, hope and love.

Yet the quest for coherence persists. And Eliot, having asked 'where', answers his question in a thousand and one ways. For our purposes, perhaps these lines from 'Dry Salvages' provide a clue:

> The river is within us, the sea is all about us;
> The sea is the land's edge also, the granite
> Into which it reaches, the beaches where it tosses
> Its hints of earlier and other creation:
> The starfish, the horseshoe crab, the whale's backbone;
> The pools where it offers to our curiosity
> The more delicate algae and the sea anemone.
> It tosses up our losses, the torn seine,
> The shattered lobsterpot, the broken oar
> And the gear of foreign dead men. The sea has many voices,
> many gods and many voices.[2]

We have certainly seen a great deal of the debris of civilisation and have peered into the starfishes of this collect here, and the horseshoe crab of that hymn there, and we have even taken apart the algae of a sermon-construction from over yonder. All this, and much more, is an offer 'to our curiosity' and there are going to be times when we can only say that it gives us 'hints of earlier and other creation' and no more. But for Eliot the sea in this poem is the source of life and it simply will not cease to flow and swell and give life. Like the disciples at the end of the Fourth Gospel when they returned to their former livelihood and discovered that even that was changed (John 21:1–19), the quest for coherence is to be begun right under our noses. The water is the source of God's life and the detail of our living in it is dependent on that never-ending source of energy and final purpose of eternal reconstruction.

SOME CRITERIA

To explore the borderlands of worship and tradition is to be faced with a great deal of this detail. It is impossible to arrange the terrain in a neat and systematic manner. But we can attempt to look at it through some kind of synthesis. We suggest five main headings.

First, *memory* is a foundation-stone for this journey. As we saw in Augustine's *Confessions*, the memory is more than just what one particular human being happens to remember at a given time. It is a deep-down source of identity for communities as well as individuals. Indeed, if we are not in touch with our tradition, we begin to suffer from amnesia. But to argue for memory is not to argue for a life of 'no-change-at-all-costs'. Indeed, one of the forces that is potentially the most destructive and at the same time potentially the most creative about what is going on in the churches today is exactly this tension between change and stability. In the liturgy, we have (most of us) lived through an era of huge change in the outward forms of our worship. Perhaps some of this was done in too much of a hurry; certainly the production of new English-language texts could have benefited from more time. But to pretend that the past never happened is a dangerous exercise, for to enter any religious community is at once to be faced with some kind of tradition. Sometimes one is faced with paradoxes here: I can vividly remember coming across far more fragile conservatism in a supposedly 'radical' group than in a congregation worshipping in a medieval building.

There is no doubt that the power of 'iteration' in worship provides an important means of expressing stability, and one of the ventures underway in many churches at the present time is to achieve some kind of balance between those elements in worship which can vary and those which can only vary by harming that stability. The collective memory itself can vary from one place to another, which poses problems even – or especially – in the Roman Catholic Church, because this memory is about catholicity. But memory is even more subtle a part of the scenery, for what is hidden away in one age will be taken out and admired in another. We saw this process at work in Andrewes' defence of the Early Fathers as providing a special ointment at a time when there were those who wished to march onwards, right past them, in order to create something radically different. As George Guiver has recently written, 'depth psychotherapy has established beyond doubt how important it is for us to be in touch with our own past childhood.'[3]

Secondly, the *heart* has recurred as the chief motivating force of the human being's quest for meaning. Augustine loved to 'return to the heart'; Alcuin wrote a collect about the open heart; Gertrude herself wrote movingly of this process as a way of being true to oneself and what God wanted; Andrewes, like her, all but quoted Augustine when speaking of the need for spiritual guidance; Grundtvig's heart beat passionately as he almost placed 'feeling' above 'knowledge' as an apprehension of divine truth; and Rossetti opened her heart to experiences of pain as well as love.

More examples could be given, but the sum of them is to suggest that worship and tradition are fed by a sense of the true self. By that is meant, once more, the community as well as the individual. Alcuin himself lived with that tension through the very prayers which he wrote, in one place for public worship and in another place for private devotion, and he perhaps saw this most tenderly in writing his prayers for a mass for the gift of tears. But the one is meaningless without the other, for a whole Church needs a sense of its selfhood, its identity, as a mark of its maturity and openness to others. This does not mean taking everything in, for a single person or a single community cannot embrace all that may be given it, otherwise indigestion follows! The heart, however, is where the Christian appeal ultimately lies, which perhaps explains why Jesus, after having let Peter deny him three times while awaiting trial (John 18:15ff), later asked him 'do you *love* me?' after the lakeside breakfast (John 21:15–19). Liturgical change is more than the production of texts, it is the digestion of them in the heart through prayer.

Thirdly, *bricolage* is a term used by some anthropologists to describe the process by which different elements of a way of life come together and form a coherent whole. This can either take place because these different ingredients spontaneously attract each other, like the way the grand 'basilican' Eucharist of the fifth century gradually migrated to become the side-altar mass of the Carolingian period in the ninth. Or else it can happen because someone actually decides that this is how things are going to be, as with the many sources that went into the production of the first English Book of Common Prayer in 1549. But however the decisions are made, and they are usually a mixture of spontaneity and authority, the point of the story is that the Church is not a data-processing unit, constantly amassing never-ending piles of information.

Perhaps living with such a paradox is a very twentieth-century part of the landscape. We know so much more in terms of facts about past ages than did our predecessors, for example, in the sixteenth century. We know more about what church life and worship was like in the early centuries, although these are necessarily liable to different kinds of interpretation, some arguing for continuities, others for variation in local contexts.[4] Yet side-by-side this growing pile of information and interpretation in our libraries and seminar-rooms, there has grown up a generation of people many of whom care nothing about the past, let alone about how the past has become the present. What our writers can tell us is that tradition stands at the line of tension between the information about the past and the beating heart of the present. Perhaps the best example of this sifting, reflective process is in Andrewes, who could see through the mass of detail in order to view things whole. But the crucial dynamic of bricolage is that it always surrounds worship and turns the set libretto into the many diverse elements that make up an actual celebration.

Fourthly, *conflict* is always going to be part of the surrounding groundwork. Not one of our writers sat entirely easily with the Church and society around them. With the possible exception of Alcuin, they all had problems and controversies about their work. There never has been an age in which the Church somehow 'settled down'; if it did, then something was wrong! If we look at our writers, we can see behind their written and spoken words civilisations all the time breaking up and giving birth to something new. For Augustine, it was the collapse of the Roman Empire. For Alcuin, it was a new European consciousness, in which he took a vital part. For Aquinas it was a new and at first sight more 'secular' approach to expressing divine truth, as creation tranformed. For Gertrude, it was the nervousness of a new religious community growing up in an unstable environment, long after her death having to move on to new premises after the destruction of the convent at Helfta. For Andrewes, it was the new world of Protestant Britain coming to terms with the past and balancing continuity with discontinuity. For Grundtvig, it was nineteenth-century Denmark searching for a new identity after catastrophic wars. For Neale, it was nineteenth-century England trying to break away, for all the greatness of empire, from its provincial shell. And for Rossetti, it was the first real stirrings of the women's movement, sitting out personal tragedy and insisting that there is – after all – an answer.

Conflict in worship, of course, usually centres on the tension between the need for variety and the need for stability, when it is not concerned with specific innovations or recoveries from the forgotten past. But there is a much more important aspect to this quest, which we saw particularly in Augustine, Grundtvig and Rossetti. Each of them, but more explicitly Grundtvig and Rossetti, is concerned with the darker side of human experience as something which is real and not to be ignored. Grundtvig once wrote a hymn entitled, '*Er du modfallen, kaere ven*' ('Are you downcast, dear friend?'),[5] which is usually sung to a melody written by the Danish composer, Carl Nielsen – which he subsequently made the basis for his famous *Wind Quintet*. Tradition can embody this necessary side of human experience, which includes that wrestling faith that sees ultimate truth often in terms of one of Grundtvig's favourite words, a 'riddle'.

This double-edged conflict that both probes into human darkness and can eventually become content with paradox is expressed rather pointedly by D. E. Roberts as follows:

> For the most part the Churches have not yet learned that the best way to pass from defensive rationalisations to secure faith is to let doubts, inconsistencies, confusions and rebellions come out into the open instead of using various forms of spiritual coercion to keep them hidden or to draw them from awareness altogether.[6]

Fifthly, *culture* is going to have to be an essential element in the boundaries along the road. As Paul Avis has remarked, 'Christian identity is dependent on cultural norms. It settles into the shape determined by the available ideological receptacles.'[7] Each one of our writers lived within different receptacles of the Western Christian tradition, even Thomas Aquinas and Gertrude the Great within the same century. And such a richness is an argument for wondering in amazement at just how diverse these receptacles can be. Moreover, in an ecumenical age in which the churches have travelled along converging paths in many aspects of their collective lives, it can be no surprise that many of the old divisions are fading into the past – a past which now stands in need of reinterpretation to explain how some of the mistakes arose that gave rise to those unhappy divisions.

Among our writers, there are startling examples of the ways in which the traditional divides between Catholic and Protestant have been bridged at first remove across the centuries: Augustine had a profound influence on Luther, which will have made him familiar to Grundtvig. And the East keeps breaking in, indirectly through Augustine's experiences at Milan, and Alcuin's innate suspicion of what was beyond the West in his own time; and more directly in Andrewes' own individual ecumenical enterprise, as well as more obviously in Grundtvig and Neale. Culture, it would seem, is never static. As Pierre Bourdieu pointed out some years ago, what makes culture excellent is often what he calls 'the art of necessary improvisation'.[8] He contrasts this with what he calls 'habitus', which are the norms by which what is done is originally set in motion and maintained. This kind of reciprocal relationship that provides context from text, worship in the moment from tradition as handed down, comes near to what George Steiner has recently described a '*re*-cognition, a meaningfulness which is that of a freedom of giving and of reception beyond the constraints of immanence'.[9]

Here, it would seem, we have a new kind of polarity which may assist us to understand how tradition and worship interact. Improvisation is what happens 'on the occasion' – whether it is the choice of hymns, or the spontaneous (or planned) insertions. 'Habitus' is what has been handed down and is trusted as a basic norm. But the two need each other – and that involves mutual trust and risk. It also inevitably means a sense of incompleteness, which is part of the character of immanence. Perhaps we can see these motivations at work in the Trinitarian piety of Alcuin and Gertrude, and in the powerful but intimate language of the

Holy Spirit found in Andrewes and Grundtvig. Perhaps we can even go further and suggest that this very process of 'giving and reception' is part of the nature of God.

SO WHAT IS TRADITION IN WORSHIP?

It will by now have become clear that this exploration of border-territory has assumed a fruitful relationship between Scripture, tradition, reason and experience. Such different influences are not always going to live happily together, as fashions come and go and worship has to be helped by tradition to discard or to reappropriate as people move on into new climates of living. Our survey has, moreover, been written by one formed in the Anglican tradition, but with a strong dose of Lutheran culture, and a commitment to the ecumenical venture. Perhaps this may suggest why the following guidelines seem to emerge.

First of all, tradition in worship is a resource from which choices are made. Not one of our writers has an unblemished record here, for they were all very much creatures of their context. But choices are part of life and they continue even to overwhelm people today. We want freedom to choose, but when faced with choice often want simply to be told what to do! And that holds true as much for the supermarket as for which eucharistic prayer is going to be used on a weekday morning. Who chooses and why will often be the result of a spontaneous 'feeling' that this is somehow right for this particular community; or it will be decided by someone and that will be that; or it may even result from a careful process of consultation. The sociology of power is not new. It is as old as the human race. But a resource is not a uniform, predetermined set of rules. It needs to be treated like Augustine's 'cavern', from which things are taken out and loved as well as placed inside when sparklingly new.

Then, tradition in worship is an embodiment of what people did and still do today. The word 'embodiment' gives the right human image, for when we worship we are entering a world in which others have joined in the same activity before us and others are doing so now. This means, above all, a sense of the communion of saints, not as a group of people who are some-where else and who lived in carefully graded departments at increasing distance from our own time, the only era of any significance. Of all the articles in the Apostles' Creed, to say that 'I believe in the communion of saints' is probably what slips off the tongue most frequently without any thought that it might mean something. And yet the way in which our writers have spoken on their own terms to our age suggests that they should not be viewed as distant from us, with Rossetti nearest and Augustine farthest away. As Thomas Traherne (*c*. 1636–74) observed: 'Men do mightily wrong themselves when they refuse to be present in all ages. . . By seeing the Saints of all ages we are present with them.'[10]

Next, tradition in worship provides a set of precedents but they cannot at the end of the day tell us what to do. This is one of the reasons why an age in which there is a great deal of liturgical change usually leads into another where official forms tend to become more static. Whether this pattern is going to repeat itself in the years ahead is not clear. But whatever happens, the dynamic of tradition in worship along these borderlands is going to become all the more important. If liturgical forms stabilise, then we are going to need to reflect carefully on how the stablished forms can continue to breathe life into the new civilisations ahead. On the other hand, if we are in for yet more change, then such a reflection will probably be a yet more subtle exercise, involving a listening ear and a mind attuned to how the past can yield of its best. It is not possible to determine in advance what kind of balance will result from continuity and discontinuity. But all our writers knew the game of using the set forms, conversing with them, even playing with them, in order to build up that never-ceasing debate on how to bridge the gap between what 'the tradition' is trying to say and 'where I am now.' The two women, Gertrude and Rossetti, perhaps sound the most intuitive notes here. Tradition has not been able to marginalise them.

Then there is the question, from where does the material for worship and tradition come? It is very easy for our kind of discussion to sound all too churchy, as if Augustine were simply tapping a recognised tradition of terminology, as also Alcuin with his prayers, and similarly with the others. In fact, the reverse is the case. Each one of them in their highest – and lowest – moments of creativity stared human nature in the face as they knew it in their own time and then looked at God. What resulted from that process of reflection is what we have been engaged

with in our survey. And what they saw in human nature was
nothing less than the great human issues of identity, meaning,
fear, love, remorse, creation, the heart, relationships, darkness,
openness, tragedy. It was in their capacity to bring these truths
into the orbit of worship within a living tradition that marked
them out as prophetic. In our own age, they do no more than
set in motion a similar process for us to carry out in our own
way. These issues, after all, are what actually matter to most
people.

Finally, tradition in worship does provide a series of lessons
for anyone ready to hear them. There are good things as well
as more guarded things that one can say about any one of them.
We may or may not admire Thomas Aquinas' language about
transubstantiation but it is probably just as well that this term
never entered the official prayer-forms of his church. We may
bask in Andrewes' effervescent mind, at times like a spinning-
wheel in its motions, but it is perhaps for the good that he was
not charged with rewriting the Prayer Book. We may want to
savour the deeply human emotions of Rossetti, and note their
absence from most of the other writers, but it is doubtless fortu-
itous that she did remain on those margins so that a century on
from her death she can be seen in a more objective light. But
there are two particular lessons which they offer, one positive,
the other negative. The positive lesson is about keeping eyes
both on the past and the future – for that is what tradition is
about. To know and to love the past at its best is to expect and
to love the future. The negative is related to it: and it is about
not becoming too self-obsessed. For to be so intent on the
present is to live a rootless life in which all that matters is 'me'
and 'my world' – a very *un*-Gospel attitude.

To live in tradition is about living an authentic life in which
our present is given coherence from our past, and hope from our
future. And the most usual means is by sympathetic adaptation,
which has kept recurring on our borderlands throughout these
pages, whether it is Augustine writing of memory, Alcuin composing a collect, Thomas Aquinas bringing the Eucharist into
time and history, Gertrude meditating on her heart and the
wounds of Christ, Andrewes preaching about forgiveness and
renewal, Grundtvig translating a Latin hymn, Neale looking at
the Greek liturgies, or Rossetti writing a poem for Trinity

Sunday. We cannot take in the whole picture at any given time but we can try to broaden our perspectives and widen our horizons. To live in tradition is to look further ahead – or back – than the end of one's theological nose.

WORSHIP AND THEOLOGY

None of our writers was prominent in the business of creating liturgies, with the possible exceptions of Alcuin (with his prayer-writing) and Grundtvig (with his hymnody). But they all walked these borderlands and whether they did so consciously or not, they understood how important it is for Christian faith to be expressed in ways and forms that helped people make the link between what they are doing when they are at public worship and what they are thinking and praying the rest of the time.

Often this influence on living people is by impression rather than deliberate and obvious action. I can remember being taken by my mother to hear James Stewart (1896–1990) preach in the grand neo-classical interior of St George's West Parish Church, Edinburgh. He was probably one of the greatest figures in the Church of Scotland in his day. I cannot remember a single word he spoke but what I can remember is the power and conviction with which he did speak, conveying to a teenager that life on this planet matters and that it is part of God's created order, loved and redeemed by him. He spoke with urgency. But it was not until years later that I came to know and love his best-seller on preaching, *Heralds of God*.[11] Similarly, I can remember listening to a sermon by Michael Ramsey when he once visited St Mary's Cathedral, Edinburgh, only a matter of yards from St George's West, but built in the grand Gothic Revival style. I only recall one word from the sermon – 'holiness'; and I can still remember the quaint intonation with which he uttered that word again and again. But it was not until years later that I came to know and love what was perhaps his greatest book, *The Gospel and the Catholic Church*.[12] Here were two men who were steeped in twentieth-century life – and the life of God. Here were two sons of Reformation churches, reaching out in the ecumenical enterprise in order to help foster that dynamic of worship in tradition in two such different contexts.

The Reformation arose from a series of convergent movements that wanted to draw the Catholic Church back to her

roots. The reasons and consequences are familiar. And they
bred in the various churches of the Reformation – Reformed,
Lutheran, Anglican and other – a self-conscious discernment
that what the Church is and does must be subjected to scrutiny,
in the first place by Scripture itself. But for a long time, a more
subtle discussion has been going on between the churches over
the relationshp between worship and theology. It has often relied
on the formula *lex orandi – lex credendi* ('the rule of praying –
the rule of believing'). This has been understood as a short-hand
for regarding what a community believes as being expressed in
how it prays. It has even been taken to mean, 'If you want to
know what we believe, come and see how we worship.' Such an
all-embracing approach has enabled Catholics and Protestants,
Easterners and Westerners, to appreciate each other's wares
more warmly.

In fact, this motto goes back to one of the writings of Prosper
of Aquitaine (*c.* 390–463), someone much influenced by Augustine. In one passage, he tries to argue for tradition located in
worship, where norms are established, 'so that the law of prayer
may establish a law for belief'.[13] In recent years, Alexander
Schmemann (Orthodox), Geoffrey Wainwright (Methodist) and
Aidan Kavanagh (Roman Catholic) have all contributed to the
discussion of exactly what this text means for the churches today.
Predictably, perhaps, they have emerged with similar wares,
Schmemann arguing for the equation of worship and doctrine,
Wainwright wanting to test worship by theology, and Kavanagh
asserting the need for worship to have autonomy over everything
else. It is clear that there is a grain of truth in all three interpre-
tations, for we do learn our faith from how we worship; but how
we worship does need to be tested by some kind of theological
judgement; and yet worship needs in part to float freely from
the invasions of the intellect. As Kavanagh once mused in an
aside at a lecture, 'the encounter at the burning bush was no
seminar.'

Exactly what Prosper meant is no longer important. But for
the purposes of our study, we must note just how critical tradition is in the formation of worship and how new ways of
speaking about the things of God have a habit of invading
worship all the time. They effect this invasion by attending to
the great human issues such as fear and love, tears and self-

discovery. They also work through the patterns of 'bricolage' that we noted earlier, including devotion and preaching. 'Affective' piety may have reached exotic heights in Gertrude the Great's writings and Andrewes' devotions, but it is still very much alive in our own time, and one wonders if the treasures of the past could be further explored and brought out into the light of today. Similarly, preaching may have been superlative in the hands of Andrewes himself, but sermons are still being delivered today which stand in need of being consciously located in a tradition. The law of worship has a task to perform in establishing the way people express what they believe, even when mistakes or exaggerations result. Worship and tradition therefore need to live in perpetual courtship, like two butterflies in love with each other.

PROSPECT

> After this, I looked, and lo, in heaven an open door! And the first voice, which I had heard speaking to me like a trumpet, said, 'Come up hither, and I will show you what must take place after this' (Rev. 4:1).

For many centuries, this passage with its vision of the 24 elders in heaven has been read for the epistle on Trinity Sunday and it is not hard to see why.[14] At a dramatic moment in the unfolding of the book of Revelation, as John Sweet says, 'John has moved into heaven where past, present and future exist as one whole.'[15] And George Caird supplies the next clue to the significance of this vision: 'John knows that to ordinary mortals the presence of God becomes real not through direct vision, even in the mind's eye, but through the impact of those to whom God is the supreme reality. So he allows his readers to look on the Eternal Light through the mirror of the worshipping host of heaven.'[16]

In a sense this is what we have been trying to do in a more mundane way in our study so far, namely to create a vision for drawing past and present together against a background of a future, God's future, which lies beyond our reach. Secondly, we have tried to do so by looking at the lives of a random selection of personalities to whom God was such a supreme reality that they could do nothing but think and write about him. Worship and tradition meet in the vision of heaven, for that is where they belong. For worship and tradition never stand still, since in God's time – eternity – they are brought together from earthly fragmentation into the unity for which they are appointed. Past, present and future exist as one whole and the Eternal Light is glimpsed through those who have gone before us.

But how can we view that Light on earth? For many people its shine will come in different ways. To revert to the examples with which our quest began, the story of redemption can be proclaimed in the grand style of Basil's eucharistic prayer, or Julian's revelation in the truth, wisdom and love of the here and now, or in God's 'secret' future as perceived by the Letter to the Ephesians. All our main writers, however, have been Western European. Let me therefore end on an Eastern note, with a story about an icon.

In the summer of 1993, Holy Trinity Church Guildford was closed for interior repairs, during which time the parish held all its worship in its other church, dedicated to St Mary the Virgin. It always strikes a pleasing chord when I hear of adjacent parish churches in town centres that are dedicated to the Trinity and the Incarnation, whether I happen to be in Cherbourg or Copenhagen. Among the work done on Holy Trinity that summer was the removal of the font from its former position in the north-west porch to a new place against the south wall. The question which occupied us was, what do we do to highlight the font in an eighteenth-century building that has its fair share of memorials?

After some discussion, we decided to commission a large icon of the baptism of Christ, to be painted by Dom Anselm Shobrook of the Anglican Benedictine community at Alton. Such an icon would have a threefold effect on the building. It would give prominence to the font at a time when baptism is receiving the attention long overdue to it in the life and worship of the community. It would help, too, to fill the nave with rich colours, not least deep gold, and create some sacred space around the font in happy dialogue with the altar. And it would also express the dedication of the church itself, for the scene of the baptism of Christ shows forth the Trinity, as Lancelot Andrewes said in his 1612 Whitsun sermon, 'The Father in the voice, the Son in the flood, the Holy Ghost in the shape of a dove.'[17] Moreover, unlike the 'triple aura' found on coinage just after Alcuin's lifetime, such a manifestation of the Trinity also symbolises the Incarnation. For here is Jesus Christ, blessing with his right hand and reaching out with his left. Here he is transforming the depths of humanity while angels and human beings look on, the angels in pure worship, while we do so (as rightly we should) in worship that is mixed with enquiry.

All this – and much more – came together in a wonderful work of art that is at once very traditional and very contemporary. The divisions of humanity which Eliot alludes to in his poetry include the fragmentation of knowledge and the debris of civilisations. These were just as dear to the hearts of Augustine and Alcuin, of Aquinas and Gertrude, of Andrewes and Grundtvig, and of Neale and Rossetti. And they are all united in form, shape and colour for twentieth-century Christians coming and going in that building, as they glimpse tradition summed up in the icon and their eyes are opened to the eternal world that is for ever being handed on to us – now.[18]

Eternal Light, shine into our hearts; eternal Goodness, deliver us from evil; eternal Power, be our support; eternal Wisdom, scatter the darkness of our ignorance; eternal Pity, have mercy on us; that with all our heart and mind and strength we may seek your face and be brought by your infinite mercy to your holy presence; through Jesus Christ our Lord. Amen.[19]

(Alcuin)

Notes

PREFACE
1. Stewart Sutherland, *Faith and Ambiguity* (London, SCM, 1984).

CHAPTER ONE: JOURNEY OF DISCOVERY
1. See, for example, Paolo Emilio Taviani, *Christopher Columbus: The Grand Design* (London, Orbis, 1985).
2. *Christian Initiation* (A Report by the Liturgical Commission of the General Synod of the Church of England) (London, Church House Publishing, 1995), p. 23.
3. *On the Way: Towards an Integrated Approach to Christian Initiation* (GS Misc 444) (London, Church House Publishing, 1995).
4. See in particular Edward Moss, *Growing into Freedom: A Way to Make Sense of Ourselves* (Guildford, Eagle, 1993).
5. The most detailed study is John R. K. Fenwick, *The Anaphoras of St Basil and St James: An Investigation into their Common Origin* (Orientalia Christiania Analecta 240) (Rome, Pontificium Institutum Orientale, 1992).
6. Text used here taken from *The Eucharistic Prayer of Saint Basil: Text for Consultation* (Washington, International Commission on English in the Liturgy, 1985), pp. 8–9. This prayer forms the basis of the Ecumenical 'Common' eucharistic prayer authorised by a number of North American churches, for which see, e.g. *The Book of Common Prayer* (New York, Seabury, 1979), pp. 372–5.
7. See *The Revelations of Divine Love of Julian of Norwich* (translated by James Walsh, S. J.) (London, Burns and Oates, 1961), p. 121. See also two recent books: Andrew Louth, *The Wilderness of God* (London, Darton, Longman & Todd, 1991), pp. 70ff; Gordon Mursell, *Out of the Deep: Prayer as Protest* (London, Darton, Longman & Todd, 1989), pp. 91ff.
8. Martin Kitchen, *Ephesians* (London, Routledge, 1994), pp. 35ff.

CHAPTER TWO: AUGUSTINE: JOURNEY INWARDS?
1. See David Silk, *Prayers for Use at the Alternative Services* (London, Mowbrays, 1980), no. 217. This is a modern version of that which appears in Frank Colquhoun, *Parish Prayers* (London, Hodder and Stoughton, 1967), no. 1602, where it is also attributed to Augustine. Whether or not all the prayers attributed to Augustine were actually written by him, Paula Clifford has produced a translation of Valeria Boldoni's collection of quotations

from his works which are direct addresses to God; see *Praying with Saint Augustine* (London, SPCK, 1987). It is interesting to note that the majority of them come from the *Confessions*.

2. *Saint Augustine: Confessions; Translated with an Introduction and Notes by Henry Chadwick* (Oxford, Clarendeon Press, 1991). Hereafter referred to as *Confessions*. See also Henry Chadwick, *Augustine* (Past Masters) (Oxford, University Press, 1986). I am indebted to Henry Chadwick for a talk he gave on Augustine to a group of friends in Guildford on 18 Oct. 1994.

3. See, e.g., J. N. D. Kelly, *Early Christian Doctrines* (London, A. & C. Black, 1958), pp. 271–9.

4. See, e.g., Thomas J. Talley, *The Origins of the Liturgical Year* (New York, Pueblo, 1986); G. G. Willis, *St Augustine's Lectionary* (Alcuin Club Collections 44) (London, SPCK, 1962).

5. See Kenneth Stevenson, *Nuptial Blessing: A Study of Christian Marriage Rites* (Alcuin Club Collections 64) (London, SPCK, 1982), pp. 29ff.

6. See the recent edition by James O'Donnell, *Augustine: Confessions* (3 vols.) (Oxford, University Press, 1992), which also discusses the structure of the work in detail. See also Peter Brown, *Augustine of Hippo: A Biography* (London, Faber, 1967), esp. pp. 180f on the relationship between the concluding books and the first nine. The seminal study of Augustine is still John Burnaby, *Amor Dei: A Study of the Religion of St Augustine* (reprint with foreword by Oliver O'Donovan) (Norwich, Canterbury Press, 1991). On the (sadly neglected) 'rule', persistently overshadowed by St Benedict's, see *The Rule of Saint Augustine* (with introduction and commentary by Tarsicius J. Van Bavel, translated by Raymond Canning) (London, Darton, Longman & Todd, 1984).

7. *Confessions* I.i (1), p. 3.

8. *Confessions* IV.xii (18), pp. 63f. The quotation from Isaiah is from the Latin translation of the Old Testament with which Augustine was familiar. It is a favourite idea in Augustine; see O'Donnell, Vol. II, p. 242, where he refers to *Ennarationes* on Pss. 57:3; 70:14 (first sermon), and Ps. 76:15, where the Isaiah quotation is given. It also appears, not as a quotation, but in a more general discussion, on Ps. 33:8 (second sermon).

9. *Confessions* X.xvii (26), p. 194. I read out part of this passage at the interment of the ashes of a friend and parishioner, Dan Crawshaw, on Easter Eve 1992. It attracted interest from his family.

10. *Confessions* XI.xx (26), p. 235.

11. *Confessions* XIII.xl (12), p. 279.

12. *De Trinitate* 10.18. Quoted from Henry Bettenson, *The Later Christian Fathers* (London, Oxford University Press, 1970), p. 235.

13. Henry Chadwick, 'Ministry and Tradition', in *Tradition and Exploration: Collected Papers on Theology and the Church* (Norwich, Canterbury Press, 1994), p. 14.

14. See Burnaby, p. 49.

15. Rowan Williams, *After Silent Centuries* (Oxford, Perpetua Press, 1994), p. 31.

CHAPTER THREE: ALCUIN OF YORK: MASTER OF ADAPTATION

1. See F. E. Brightman, *The English Rite* (Vol. 2) (London, Rivingtons, 1915), pp. 40ff, for texts in the first Prayer Books, with the Latin from the Sarum original. For the text in the original Alcuin Mass of the Holy Spirit, see

Jean Deshusses, *Le Sacramentaire Grégorien: ses principales formes d'après les plus anciens manuscrits* (Tome II) (Spicilegium Friburgense 24) (Fribourg, Editions Universitaires, 1979), no. 2325.

2. See Martin R. Dudley, *The Collect in Anglican Liturgy* (Alcuin Club Collections 72) (Collegeville, The Liturgical Press, 1994).

3. See Stephen Sykes, 'Cranmer on the open heart', in Sykes, *Unashamed Anglicanism* (London, Darton, Longman & Todd, 1995), pp. 24ff. See also Abbot Justin McCann (ed.), *The Cloud of Unknowing* (London, Burns Oates, 1924), p. 3, where the collect has been rendered into English in the first person singular, and is followed by the Latin original. In Alan Bennett's play, *The Madness of George III*, it is the collect for purity (almost!) in its Prayer Book version, which is put into the mouth of the King as he is forcibly given the first doses of his treatment.

4. See above, Chapter 2, n. 8.

5. The definitive, up-to-date life of Alcuin has yet to be written. Meanwhile, see Stephen Allott, *Alcuin of York – His Life and Letters* (York, William Sessions, 1974). See also the (somewhat dated) Andrew Fleming West, *Alcuin and the Rise of the Christian Schools* (New York, Greenwood Press, 1969) (reprint of first edition, originally published in 1892). I am also indebted to Dennis Bradley, formerly Lecturer in Classical Studies at Manchester University, for a copy of his paper, 'Alcuin's role in the Carolingian Renaissance', read to the Manson Society, 22 Feb. 1984.

6. On the masses of Alcuin, see Henri Barré and Jean Deshusses, 'A la recherche du missel d'Alcuin', *Ephemerides Liturgicae* 52 (1968), pp. 3–44; Jean Deshusses, 'les messes d'Alcuin', *Archiv für Liturgiewissenschaft* 14/1 (1972), pp. 7–41. The texts are also to be found in Deshusses, *Le Sacramentaire Grégorien* II (see footnotes). See also, e.g., Ruth A. Meyers, 'The Wisdom of God and the Word of God: Alcuin's Mass "of Wisdom" ' in Martin Dudley (ed.), *Like a Two-Edged Sword: The Word of God in Liturgy and History* (Norwich, Canterbury Press, 1995), pp. 39–59.

7. See Mary Clayton, *The Cult of the Virgin Mary in Anglo-Saxon England* (Cambridge Studies in Anglo-Saxon England 2) (Cambridge, University Press, 1990), esp. pp. 54–61. Clayton suggests that the work was written at York. It may have been the fruit of one of Alcuin's return visits, but by 790 he was definitely in the service of Charlemagne and based at Aachen. The antiphons quoted are from Clayton's own translations, see p. 56, n. 14, nos. 80, 81, 83, 95.

8. Author's translation. Many of these prayers are to be found in D. A. Wilmart's collection, *Precum Libelli Quattuor Aevi Karolini* (Prior Pars) (Rome, Ephemerides Liturgicae, 1940), which needs to be read with the Barré-Deshusses article cited above in n. 6. The prayer cited is on pp. 15f.

9. For the Trinity prayers, see Deshusses, *Le Sacramentaire Grégorien* II, nos. 1806–1810. For a discussion of the origins of the proper preface, see Antoine Chavasse, *Le Sacramentaire Gélasien* (Bibliothèque de Théologie Série IV) (Histoire de la Théologie I) (Paris, Desclée, 1957), pp. 254–62. On the development of the feast of the Trinity, see P. Browe, 'Zur Geschichte des Dreifaltigkeitsfeste', *Archiv für Liturgiewissenschaft* 1 (1959), pp. 65–81. See also, in general, Catherine Mowry LaCugna, 'Making the Most of Trinity Sunday', *Worship* 60.3 (1986), pp. 210–24. On Alcuin and the 'Fulda' books, see Eric Palazzo, *Les sacramentaires de Fulda: Etude sur l'iconographie et la liturgie à l'époque ottonienne* (Liturgiewissenschafliche Quellen und Forschungen 77) (Münster, Aschendorff, 1994), pp. 146ff.

10. See Beate Günzel, *Aelfwine's Prayer Book* (Henry Bradshaw Society 108) (London, 1993), pp. 128–31 (Office), pp. 53–5 (discussion of text, but the list of sources is incomplete). Compare what appears to be another version of this office, but which the editor thinks is a private devotion, in Bernard James Muir, *A Pre-Conquest English Prayer-Book* (Henry Bradshaw Society 103) (London, 1988), pp. 147–9.

11. A similar approach is taken in A. M. Allchin, *The Joy of all Creation: An Anglican Meditation on the Place of Mary* (London, Darton, Longman & Todd, 1984); revised edition by Dublin, New City Press, 1994.

12. See Christopher Blunt, Ian Stewart and Stewart Lyon, 'The Coinage of Southern England, 796–840', *British Numismatic Journal* 32 (1964), pp. 1–74; see in particular p. 11 and footnote. I am indebted to Stewart Lyon, former Churchwarden of Holy Trinity Church, Guildford, for drawing my attention to this; he was responsible for the 'triple aura' being fixed to the top of the Churchwardens' staves in Holy Trinity.

13. See Alcuin, '*De fide sanctae et individuae Trinitatis*' (= 'On the faith of the holy and undivided Trinity') in Migne, *Patrologia Latina* 101, 9–63. On Alcuin and the Apostles' Creed, see J. N. D. Kelly, *Early Christian Creeds* (London, Longmans, 1952), pp. 353ff.

14. For Roman Catholic text, see *The Sacramentary* (New York, Catholic Publishing Company, 1974), p. 346; for Anglican text, see *The Alternative Service Book 1980* (London, Clowes, SPCK, Cambridge University Press, 1980), p. 640.

15. On the lections, for ordinary see Deshusses, *Le Sacramentarire Grégorien* (Tome III) (Spicilegium Friburgense 28) (Fribourg, Presses Universitaires, 1982), pp. 299, 301. For the epistle for the Sunday after Pentecost, see Antoine Chavasse, *Les Lectionnaires romains de la messe au VIIè et au VIIIè siècle* (Tome II) (Spicilegii Friburgensis Subsidida 22) (Fribourg, Editions Universitaires, 1993), p. 16.

CHAPTER FOUR: TWO THIRTEENTH-CENTURY CONTRASTS: THOMAS AQUINAS AND GERTRUDE THE GREAT

1. Text in *The Scottish Book of Common Prayer* (Edinburgh, Cambridge University Press, 1929), p. 171. This is the standard 'Cranmer-style' translation that appears in various books of prayers, and it appears to be derived from the version in Orby Shipley's *Ritual of the Altar* (London, Longmans, 1878), for 'the Feast of the most holy Sacrament', presumably Corpus Christi. The prayer also appears (altered so that it addresses the Father) in *The Alternative Service Book 1980*, p. 920, in 'Thanksgiving for the Institution of Holy Communion'.

2. For the life and thought of Thomas, see James A. Weisheipl, *Friar Thomas D'Aquino* (Oxford, Blackwell, 1974).

3. See Martin Dudley, 'Liturgy and Doctrine: Corpus Christi', in *Worship* 66.5 (1992), pp. 417–26.

4. Translation taken from *Saint Andrew Daily Missal* (Bruges, Biblica, 1962), pp. 627ff. See Bernard Capelle, 'les oraisons de la messe du saint sacrement', *Travaux Liturgiques* III (Louvain, Abbaye du Mont César, 1967), pp. 242–51.

5. First quotation from *Sententiae* IV.xii.2 (2, 2, ad 4); second quotation from *Sententiae* I.xxvii.3 (2, ad 1). From translation in Darwell Stone, *A History of the Doctrine of the Holy Eucharist* (Vol. I) (London, Longmans, 1909),

pp. 326f, 331. On Aquinas' eucharistic theology, see David N. Power, *The Eucharistic Mystery: Revitalizing the Tradition* (New York, Crossroad, 1992), pp. 208–40. See also Henry Chadwick, 'Ego Berengarius', in Chadwick, *Tradition and Exploration: Collected Papers on Theology and the Church* (Norwich, Canterbury Press, 1994), pp. 33–60 (reprinted from *Journal of Theological Studies* 40.2 (1989), pp. 414–45), for the background to the medieval debate in the context of Berengar, and leading on to Aquinas.

6. Geoffrey Wainwright, *Eucharist and Eschatology* (London, Epworth, 1971).

7. Richard Hooker, *Laws of Ecclesiastical Polity*, Book V, 67.11.

8. *The Whole Works of Jeremy Taylor* (edited by Reginald Heber, revised and corrected by Charles Eden) (Vol. III) (London, Longmans, 1852), p. 371. A quotation from *Holy Living* (1650).

9. See Maurice Frost, *Historical Companion to Hymns Ancient and Modern* (London, Clowes, 1962), pp. 343f.

10. See Gertrude the Great, *The Herald of God's Loving-Kindness* (Books One and Two) (translated and annotated by Alexandra Barratt) (The Cistercian Fathers Series 35) (Kalamazoo, Cistercian Publications, 1991), p. 109. Hereafter referred to as *The Herald*.

11. I am indebted to Martin Kitchen for the German translation and several observations on Gertrude's piety.

12. In addition to Alexandra Barratt's introduction, see also the following: Pierre Doyère, *Gertrude d'Helfta: Oeuvres Spirituelles: II Le Héraut* (Livres I–II) (Sources Chrétiennes 139) (Paris, Cerf, 1968); Caroline Walker Bynum, *Jesus as Mother: Studies in the Spirituality of the High Middle Ages* (Berkeley, University of California Press, 1984), pp. 170–209; Cipriano Vagaggini, *Theological Dimensions of the Liturgy* (Collegeville, Liturgical Press, 1976), pp. 740–803; Power, *The Eucharistic Mystery*, pp. 197–200.

13. *The Herald*, Ch. 15.2 (p. 140) and Ch. 21.3 (p. 158). The references to 'returning to my heart' are in Ch. 3.1 (p. 106) and Ch. 14.3 (p. 136). See Augustine, *Confessions* IV.xii (18), p. 63; discussed above in Chapter 2, n. 8.

14. *The Herald*, Ch. 4.3 (p. 110).

15. Translation from *St Andrew Daily Missal*, p. 1626. (This mass-prayer has not survived into the 1970 Missal.) See Richard W. Pfaff, *New Liturgical Feasts in Later Medieval England* (Oxford Theological Monographs) (Oxford, Clarendon Press, 1970), pp. 84–91. The end of this collect provided the inspiration for Cranmer's conclusion to the commemoration of the departed in the 1549 Eucharist; this did not survive into 1552, but the Scottish Liturgies kept it, down to the 1929 Prayer Book. See Brightman, *The English Rite* (Vol. 2), p. 690 and *The Scottish Book of Common Prayer*, p. 318.

16. *Revelations of Divine Love* (translated by Walsh), pp. 87f (Ch. 24).

17. On incense-grains, see A. J. MacGregor, *Fire and Light in the Western Triduum: Their Use at Tenebrae and at the Paschal Vigil* (Alcuin Club Collections 71) (Collegeville, Liturgical Press, 1992), pp. 339ff.

18. On Baxter, see *The Saints' Everlasting Rest*, Part 4, Ch. IX, section V, in W. Orme (ed.), *The Practical Works of Richard Baxter* (Vol. XXIII) (London, Duncan, 1830), p. 352. See also Gordon Wakefield, *Puritan Devotion* (London, Epworth, 1957), p. 99ff. I am indebted to Gordon Wakefield for drawing my attention to this.

19. *Historical Companion to Hymns Ancient and Modern*, p. 260.

CHAPTER FIVE: LANCELOT ANDREWES: PREACHER EXTRAORDINARY

1. *The Sermons of Lancelot Andrewes* III (Library of Anglo-Catholic Theology) (Oxford, Parker, 1843), p. 22. Hereafter referred to as *The Sermons* with volume number.

2. For the life of Andrewes, see Robert Ottley, *Lancelot Andrewes* (London, Methuen, 1894); Paul Welsby, *Lancelot Andrewes 1555–1626* (London, SPCK, 1958).

3. Full text in *The Sermons* V, pp. 82–103. See Kenneth Stevenson, ' "Human Nature Honoured": Absolution in Lancelot Andrewes', in *Like a Two-Edged Sword: The Word of God in Liturgy and History*, pp. 113–37. See also Kenneth Stevenson, *Covenant of Grace Renewed: A Vision of the Eucharist in the Seventeenth Century* (London, Darton, Longman & Todd, 1994), pp. 39–66.

4. Translation by David Scott, Colin Bradley and Kenneth Stevenson. The original version has only one 'I believe', at the beginning. See *The Preces Privatae of Lancelot Andrewes: Translated with an Introduction and Notes by F. E. Brightman* (London, Methuen, 1903), p. 92 (his translation) and pp. 330f (notes and parallels with sermons). The references are to *The Sermons* V, p. 462 – all four on the same page.

5. Marianne Dorman, *The Sermons of Lancelot Andrewes: Volume One; Nativity, Lenten and Passion* (Edinburgh, Pentland Press, 1992); *Volume Two: Pashcal and Pentecostal* (Edinburgh, Pentland Press, 1993); P. E. Hewson, *Select Writings of Lancelot Andrewes* (Manchester, Carcanet Press, 1995).

6. T. S. Eliot, *Essays Ancient and Modern* (London, Faber, 1936), p. 26.

7. See *The Sermons* I, pp. 249–64, and T. S. Eliot, *Collected Poems, 1909–1962* (London, Faber, 1963), pp. 109ff. I am indebted to John Lees and John Hart for assistance with Eliot here.

8. Nicholas Lossky, *Lancelot Andrewes the Preacher (1555–1626): The Origins of the Mystical Theology of the Church of England* (Oxford, Clarendon Press, 1991), p. 345.

9. *The Sermons* I, pp. 215–32.

10. *The Sermons* III, pp. 3–22.

11. *The Sermons* III, pp. 280–300. The author preached at the Winchester Cathedral Evensong on 1 Feb. 1995 on this sermon. For 'return to the heart', see on Augustine, Chapter 2, n. 8.

12. See Brightman, *The Preces Privatae*, 70, lines 31–33 and p. 65, lines 22–27.

13. Francis Paget, *The Spirit of Discipline* (London, Longmans, 1933), p. 324.

14. See Lossky, *Lancelot Andrewes*, pp. 221ff.

15. A. M. Allchin, 'Lancelot Andrewes' in Geoffrey Rowell (ed.), *The English Religious Tradition and the Genius of Anglicanism* (Wantage, Ikon Books, 1992), pp. 145–64.

CHAPTER SIX: NIKOLAI GRUNDTVIG: HYMN-WRITER
EXTRAORDINARY

1. Translation by C. Doving. Original nine-verse text in *Grundtvigs Sang-Vaerk til Den Danske Kirke* I (Copenhagen, Det Danske Forlag, 1944), no. 22, pp. 79–81. (Hereafter referred to as *GSV* with volume number. This is the reprint of the original editions of this five-volume work, published between 1837 and 1872, with three additional volumes on the text-traditions and the sources. Volumes II–V were published in 1946, 1948,

1949 and 1951, and the additional volumes on the text-traditions, with sources, in 1956, 1961 and 1964.) The current Danish hymn-book has a seven-verse version, but this 'official' English translation in fact omits verse 4. See *Den Danske Salmebog* (Copenhagen, Haase, 1952), no. 280. (Hereafter referred to as *DDS*.)

2. See *Meddelelser fra Arhus Stift* (Århus, Udgivet af Landemødet, 1966), pp. 26–30; and *Det Ny Testamente, Gengivet af Danske Digtere* (redigeret af Biskop Skat Hoffmeyer og Sognepraest Alfred Blenker. Illustreret af danske Kunstnere) (København, Werstermanns Forlag, 1944).

3. P. G. Lindhardt, *Grundtvig: An Introduction* (London, SPCK, 1951); A. M. Allchin, 'N. F. S. Grundtvig: The Spirit as Life-Giver', in *The Kingdom of Love and Knowledge: The Encounter between Orthodoxy and the West* (London, Darton, Longman & Todd, 1979), pp. 71–89. On the Danish side, there are Christian Thodberg and Anders Pontoppidan Thyssen, eds., *N. F. S. Grundtvig: Tradition and Renewal* (Copenhagen, Det Danske Selskab, 1983) and *A Grundtvig Anthology: Selections from the Writings of N. F. S. Grundtvig (1783–1872)* (Cambridge, James Clarke, 1984). The recent symposium is A. M. Allchin, D. Japser, J. H. Schjørring, and K. Stevenson, eds., *Heritage and Prophecy: Grundtvig and the English-Speaking World* (Århus, University Press, 1993 and Norwich, Canterbury Press, 1993).

4. *Evangelisk-Luthersk Psalmebog for de dansktalende Menigheder I Slesvig* (Schleswig, Bergas, 1889). Use of this book, even against the hymn-book used in Denmark itself, became a mark of Danishness.

5. See Christian Thodberg, essays in *N. F. S. Grundtvig: Tradition and Renewal*, pp. 123–96. See also his essay, 'The Importance of Baptism in Grundtvig's View of Christianity', and Kenneth Stevenson's essay, 'Grundtvig's Hymns from an Anglican Point of View', in *Heritage and Prophecy*, pp. 133–52, 153–70.

6. *DDS*, no. 418. See also *GSV* I, no. 100 (1837); IV, no. 41 (1844); V, no. 179 (1862), no. 259 (1862–3), and no. 268 (1864). The translation provided was made for the Grundtvig Seminar at St Chad's College, Durham, 5 April 1991. It was used at Morning Prayer during the meeting, and also at the Guildford Diocesan Clergy Conference, 5 Sept. that year.

7. Translation taken from Robert F. Taft, S.J., *The Great Entrance: A History of the Transfer of Gifts and other Preanaphoral Rites of the Liturgy of St John Chrysostom* (Orientalia Christiana Analecta 200) (Rome, Pontificium Institutum Studiorum Orientalium, 1975), p. 55. For the origins of the hymn, see pp. 76f. For a discussion of Grundtvig's Greek translations, see Jørgen Elbeck, *Grundtvig og de Graeske Salmer* (Copenhagen, Gad, 1960).

8. *Historical Companion to Hymns Ancient and Modern*, pp. 346f.

9. *GSV* I, no. 216. The hymn does not appear in *DDS*. It is in an awkward metre. On Grundtvig's translations, see A. M. Allchin, 'Grundtvig's translations from the Greek', *Eastern Churches Quarterly* 13/3–4 (1959), pp. 129–43.

10. *GSV* I, no. 348. *DDS*, no. 249, where verses 2, 3 and 7 of the original do not appear. See also Digby Wrangham, *The Liturgical Poetry of Adam of St Victor*, Vol. 2 (London, Kegan, Paul, Trench, 1881), pp. 100ff. Cf. the paraphrase–translation of the same hymn by William Blew (1808–94), in his *Church Hymn and Tune Book* (London, Rivingtons, 1855), no. 92, and which also appears in Orby Shipley's *Lyra Messianica* (London, Longman, 1865), no. 125 (pp. 402–5).

11. On this particular point, see the essay by J. R. Watson, 'Grundtvig and the English Hymn', in *Heritage and Prophecy*, pp. 115–32.
12. *DDS*, nos. 279, 280, 407, 415, 418, 426, 488.
13. A. M. Allchin, 'Grundtvig and England: An Introduction', in *Heritage and Prophecy*, p. 16. See also A. M. Allchin, 'The Hymns of N. F. S. Grundtvig', in *Eastern Churches Quarterly* 13.3/4 (1959), pp. 129–43.
14. I would like to express my indebtedness to J. H. Schjørring, in particular to his two works, *Grundtvig og Påsken* (Copenhagen, Gad, 1987) and *Grundtvigs Billedsprog og Den Kirkelige Anskuelse* (Frederiksberg, Anis, 1990).

CHAPTER SEVEN: TWO NINETEENTH-CENTURY CONTRASTS: JOHN
MASON NEALE AND CHRISTINA ROSSETTI

1. On the history of this hymn, see Joseph Connolly, *Hymns of the Roman Liturgy* (London, Longmans, 1957), pp. 42f, and *Historical Companion to Hymns Ancient and Modern*, p. 134.
2. See, e.g. Robert F. Taft, S. J., *The Liturgy of the Hours in East and West: The Origins of the Divine Office and its Meaning for Today* (Collegeville, Liturgical Press, 1986).
3. See Eleanor A. Towle, *John Mason Neale, D.D. A Memoir* (London, Longmans, 1906).
4. Leon Litvack, *J. M. Neale and the Quest for Sobornost* (Oxford, Clarendon, 1994).
5. See Neale's *Church Enlargement and Church Arrangement* (Cambridge, University Press, 1843).
6. *The Liturgies of S. Mark, S. James, S. Clement, S. Chrysostom, and the Church of Malabar* (translated by J. M. Neale) (London, Hayes, 1859).
7. J. M. Neale, *Essays on Liturgiology and Church History* (London, Saunders, Otley, 1863). I am also indebted to Martin Stringer for his paper on Neale's liturgical work, delivered to the Meeting of the Society of Liturgical Study, Oxford, 2 Sept. 1992.
8. See J. M. Neale, *Mediaeval Hymns and Sequences* (London, Masters, 1867) (3rd edition), pp. 18–22, where Neale appends notes on different Latin versions. For Grundtvig, see *GSV* I, no. 349, pp. 614–15, where the original 8–verse version appears. But in 1857, these were reduced to 5, *GSV* V, no. 98, pp. 178f, which the current Danish hymn-book reproduces, *DDS*, no. 289.
9. See J. M. Neale, *Hymns of the Eastern Church* (London, Hayes, 1862), pp. 20–21; *The Lenten Triodion*, translated from the original Greek by Mother Mary and Archimandrite Kallistos Ware (London, Faber, 1978), pp. 545–6. Original Greek in *Triodion* (Venice, Phoenix, 1863), pp. 363f. For a discussion of Neale's translations of other Greek hymns, see Litvack, *J. M. Neale and the Quest for Sobornost*, pp. 117–53.
10. See Kenneth Stevenson, ' "The Unbloody Sacrifice": The Origins and development of a Description of the Eucharist' in Gerard Austin (ed.), *Fountain of Life: In Memory of Niels K. Rasmussen, O.P.* (Washington, Pastoral Press, 1991), pp. 103–30.
11. See *Mediaeval Hymns and Sequences*, pp. 178–81.
12. Christina Rossetti, 'Passing Away', in Arthur Quiller-Couch, *The Oxford Book of English Verse: 1250–1900* (Oxford, Clarendon Press, 1900), no. 784, pp. 851f.

13. Jan Marsh, *Christina Rossetti: A Literary Biography* (London, Jonathan Cape, 1994). On 'Passing Away', see pp. 267, 357.
14. See Christina Rossetti, *Verses* (London, SPCK, 1893), pp. 82f.
15. *The Poems of George Herbert* (with an Introduction by Arthur Waugh) (London, Oxford University Press, 1955), p. 60. I am indebted to Stephen Sykes for drawing my attention to this poem.
16. *Verses*, pp. 146f. Quoted in Marsh, *Christina Rossetti*, p. 568.
17. See text in Frank Colquhoun, *Parish Prayers*, no. 1556, p. 372.

CHAPTER EIGHT: DRAWING ON

1. The opening lines of 'Choruses from "The Rock" ', T. S. Eliot, *Collected Poems 1909–1962* (London, Faber, 1963), p. 161.
2. ibid., pp. 205f.
3. George Guiver, *Faith in Momentum: The Distinctiveness of the Church* (London, SPCK, 1990), p. 100.
4. See, e.g., Paul F. Bradshaw, *The Search for the Origins of Christian Worship: Sources and Methods for the Study of the Early Liturgy* (London, SPCK, 1992).
5. *DDS*, no. 511. See also *GSV* IV, no. 210 (1850/1).
6. See D. E. Roberts, *Psychotherapy and the Christian View of Man* (New York, 1950), p. 71; quoted by Robert Davidson, *The Courage to Doubt: Exploring an Old Testament Theme* (London, SCM, 1983), p. 17.
7. Paul Avis, *Anglicanism and the Christian Church* (Edinburgh, T. & T. Clark, 1989), p. 302.
8. Pierre Bourdieu, *Outline of a Theory of Practice* (Cambridge, University Press, 1977), p. 214, n. 1, quoted in David F. Ford, 'What Happens in the Eucharist?', a paper for the Society for the Study of Theology, Durham 1995.
9. George Steiner, *Real Presences: Is there anything in what we say?* (London, Faber, 1989), p. 50.
10. *The Centuries of Meditations by Thomas Traherne* (edited by Bertram Doble) (London, Doble, 1908), p. 64 (Century I.85).
11. James S. Stewart, *Heralds of God: The Warrack Lectures* (London, Hodder and Stoughton, 1956).
12. Arthur Michael Ramsey, *The Gospel and the Catholic Church* (London: Longmans, 1936). See Rowan Williams, 'Theology and the Churches', in Robin Gill and Lorna Kendall (eds.), *Michael Ramsey as Theologian* (London, Darton, Longman & Todd, 1995), pp. 9–28 for an important essay evaluating Ramsey's theology of the Church.
13. Prosper of Aquitaine, *Capitula Coelestini* 8. See also Alexander Schmemann, *Introduction to Liturgical Theology* (New York, St Vladimir's Press, 1975); Geoffrey Wainwright, *Doxology: The Praise of God in Worship, Doctrine and Life* (London, Epworth, 1980); Aidan Kavanagh, *On Liturgical Theology* (New York, Pueblo, 1984). In connection with this discussion, see Maxwell Johnson, 'Liturgy and Theology', in Paul Bradshaw and Bryan Spinks (eds.), *Liturgy in Dialogue: Essays in Memory of Ronald Jasper* (London, SPCK, 1993), pp. 202–25.
14. Antoine Chavasse, *Les lectionnaires romains de la messe au VIIè et au VIIIè siècle* (Tome I), p. 59. The passage is Rev. 4:1–7, 9–12.
15. John Sweet, *Revelation* (TPI New Testament Commentaries) (London, SCM, 1990), p. 115.

16. G. B. Caird, *The Revelation of St John the Divine* (New Testament Commentaries) (London, A. & C. Black, 1966), p. 63, quoted by Sweet, p. 116.
17. *The Sermons* III, p. 199.
18. The icon inspired the composition of a short 'Office of the Trinity' using traditional and modern elements, in the style of the Morning and Evening Prayer contained in *Celebrating Common Prayer: A Version of the Daily Office, SSF* (London, Mowbrays, 1992).
19. The prayer is attributed to Alcuin of York. See Silk, *Prayers for Use at the Alternative Services*, no. 106; traditional language version in Colquhoun, *Parish Prayers*, no. 1536.

Index